MERCURY
RADIO ARTS

ALSO BY GLENN BECK

CONTROL

EXPOSING THE TRUTH ABOUT GUNS

Written and Edited by

GLENN BECK, KEVIN BALFE, AND HANNAH BECK

Writing and Research

Dan Andros, Lt. Col. Dave Grossman, Stephen Halbrook,
David Kopel, John Lott

Contributors

Sharon Ambrose, Cam Edwards, Joe Kerry, Tim McGinnis,
Skip Patel, Meg Storm and Jacob Sullum

Illustrations

Paul E. Nunn

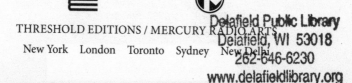

THRESHOLD EDITIONS / MERCURY RADIO ARTS

New York   London   Toronto   Sydney   New Delhi

THRESHOLD EDITIONS/MERCURY RADIO ARTS
A Division of Simon & Schuster, Inc.
1230 Avenue of the Americas
New York, NY 10020

First Threshold Editions/Mercury Radio Arts
trade paperback edition April 2013

THRESHOLD EDITIONS and colophon are
trademarks of Simon & Schuster, Inc.

For information about special discounts for bulk purchases,
please contact Simon & Schuster Special Sales at
1-866-506-1949 or business@simonandschuster.com.

The Simon & Schuster Speakers Bureau can bring authors
to your live event. For more information or to book an event,
contact the Simon & Schuster Speakers Bureau at
1-866-248-3049 or visit our website at www.simonspeakers.com.

Designed by Joy O'Meara

Manufactured in the United States of America

1   3   5   7   9   10   8   6   4   2

ISBN 978-1-4767-3987-8
ISBN 978-1-4767-3988-5 (ebook)

To Martin Luther King, Jr.

who preached nonviolence but knew that passive resistance could not be relied on for his own family's protection. King owned several guns but was subjected to the worst kind of gun control—and deprived of his basic right to defend himself and his family—when police in Alabama denied him a concealed carry permit in 1956. When will we learn? The right to bear arms shall not be infringed.

CONTENTS

CONTENTS

PART TWO: Winning Hearts and Minds

AUTHOR'S NOTE

We can do better. We must do something.

—SENATOR RICHARD BLUMENTHAL (D-CT),
December 20, 2012

We must act, we must act, we must act.

—ARNE DUNCAN, U.S. secretary of education, January 26, 2013

L ast December a man was pushed onto the subway tracks in midtown Manhattan. He was hit by a train as he struggled to pull himself back up onto the platform.

Fifty-five people were killed by New York City subway trains in 2012, but this incident stood out for one major reason: a freelance photographer who'd been standing on the platform snapped a photo of the man just seconds before he was struck. The next morning the photo appeared on the front page of the *New York Post*.

With the horrific image in hand, the media had a story. *This was now an epidemic.* Every time someone got hit, the incident was treated as though it were another example of just how lethal the New York City subway had become. And, of course, politicians demanded action. "We cannot have incident after incident take place like this without saying we are going to act," said Councilman James Vacca as he called for an emergency hearing. "We have to have a plan."

And so a plan was crafted: glass walls could be built from floor to ceiling along the tracks of all 468 stations in the system. Accidents would be stopped and suicidal people would have to find another way to kill themselves. It would big, audacious, and expensive—and it would send a signal to everyone that this epidemic of violence would not be tolerated.

There was only one small problem with all of this: there was no epidemic. In fact, *fewer* people had been struck by trains that year than the year before, and the number of fatalities was right around the five-year average. The front-page photos and increased media attention had clouded public perception, but the statistics did not lie.

It's human nature to want to do something when confronted with a tragedy. It makes us feel good. It makes us sleep better. It makes people vote for us.

But it often doesn't make a real difference.

There have been several unthinkable tragedies involving guns recently. The media and many politicians tell us that these massacres are happening more frequently than ever before; that America is the most violent country on earth; that our schools are unsafe; that semi-automatic assault rifles are to blame; and that *we must do something.*

As you'll discover in this book, the basic premise of every single one of those claims is wrong. Worse, when we allow these myths to be accepted as fact, we end up focusing so much on the *how* of these crimes—the weapon itself—that we stop ourselves from asking the far more appropriate question: *why?*

Last year in New York City a nanny stabbed to death the two young children she was caring for. It was a gruesome, traumatic incident that shocked the entire city. In the aftermath of this tragedy, the media focused on the nanny's background, trying desperately to figure out her motive. Everyone wanted to know if there was something that should have tipped people off or some way to prevent this from ever happening again.

But no one talked about the knife. People intuitively understood that this woman could have used a knife, a gun, or her bare hands—the weapon didn't really matter; it was just a tool. What mattered was not the how—horrific as it was—but the *why.*

Unfortunately, when it comes to guns, this kind of sober analysis is usually turned upside down. After someone is shot, the story starts with details about the kind of gun used, the capacity of its magazine, and a rundown of how it was acquired. The *why* comes later and, even then, we usually hear only what we want to hear. It's easy when the motive fits our preconceived notions— revenge, greed, money, sex, or drugs—but what about when it doesn't? What happens when we uncover that some of the worst juvenile killers in our history were influenced—and in some cases, *trained,* by entertainment violence, like video games? Do we continue to ask questions and pursue the truth, or do we stop listening because it hits so close to home?

On a Sunday night in December, two days after the Newtown, Connecticut, school massacre (a massacre perpetrated by a boy who reportedly had an obsession with violent video games), David Axelrod, the president's former top political adviser, was watching a football game and posted an observation on Twitter: "In NFL postgame: an ad for shoot 'em up video game. All for curbing weapons of war. But shouldn't we also quit marketing murder as a game?"

I'm sure that David Axelrod and I don't agree on much, but the answer to his question, as you'll see in Part Two of this book, is an unequivocal *yes*. The evidence is indisputable that what is different in society now isn't the guns; it's the person, the culture, and the cavalier way we treat violence. Without morality and virtue most things in a free society fall apart. But with them, anything is possible.

Of course, that argument is not going to satisfy everyone—especially those who are predisposed to blaming guns for everything. So, in Part One, I go through all the myths and lies that have been told about guns and the Second Amendment over the last few months and dismantle them, point by point. For example, gun-related mass killings are, thankfully, still incredibly rare. As with the New York City subway incidents, there has been no increase in the frequency of these events, or the number of people who die in them. What has increased, however, is the number of people making the case that Americans should give back some of their liberty in an attempt to buy a little security.

I think I remember someone pretty smart once advising that those who do that deserve neither liberty nor security.

The Founders wrote in the Second Amendment that our right to keep and bear arms "shall not be infringed." To *infringe* means "to limit or undermine"—so you'll have to forgive me for being a little skeptical about those who use a tragedy to promote an agenda that culminates in limiting or undermining our right to keep and bear arms. Besides, the people who talk most about the need to regulate guns are also usually the same people who know the least about them. Ask these gun prohibitionists about the Second Amendment and they'll usually mention hunting or sport shooting. I've searched and searched the Constitution and can't find any mention of how our ability to shoot deer or quail is pertinent to securing the "blessings of liberty."

In my view, the right to bear arms is in the Constitution for three main reasons: self-protection, community protection, and protection from tyranny. Because those are such large, overarching intentions, they're virtually impossible to destroy all at once. So progressives start small. They introduce "commonsense" regulations and restrictions that will supposedly save lives. Then, each time the public's attention is captured, they push further. Given enough time, guns and ammunition will eventually become so costly and time-consuming to purchase, maintain, and insure that a ban will no longer be necessary.

And that's what this is really all about: control. Not of guns, but of *us*. Controlling what we eat and drive, how we heat our homes, and how we educate our kids—that's all small potatoes compared to controlling our overall relationship with government. If progressives can change the Second Amendment from "shall not be infringed" to "no guns except what we allow," then they will have turned the entire Constitution on its head.

This is the path we are on. The only way to change our course is to expose this agenda and wake as many people up as possible. That is one of the reasons I published this book in this format: I wanted it to be inexpensive and easily shareable. It's my hope that you will read it and then pass it on to others, especially those who may be susceptible to trading away their liberty in a time of crisis.

I am a proud gun owner and lifetime member of the NRA. I believe firmly that our Bill of Rights is not merely a list of suggestions, but a road map to freedom. When we stray from that map even a little, and even for what seems to be a very good reason, we are certain to face the consequences.

So go ahead and arm yourself with a gun—learn how to use it safely and always respect what it represents—but I hope that you'll also arm yourself and your family with the one thing that's even more powerful: information. Know the facts. Live the truth.

Information is power. Those without it have nothing. Those with it
will always have CONTROL.

Glenn Beck
Dallas, Texas
March 2013

PART ONE

The Truth about Guns

After the Newtown massacre in December 2012 it quickly became obvious that gun control was again going to take over the national dialogue. The president, who had barely used the word *gun* over his first four years in office, was about to rearrange his second-term agenda. Gun control would now be right near the top of the priority list.

Sensing a once-in-a-generation opportunity, controllist politicians and groups began to pounce. News programs devoted full hours to the issue. Opinion hosts like Piers Morgan, sensing an issue to make their mark with, began virtual crusades, discussing the topic nightly. Hollywood celebrities, brought together by the progressive group Mayors Against Illegal Guns, "demanded a plan" to end gun violence via YouTube videos and television commercials. This, of course, despite that fact that many of those who appeared in the videos had made their careers—and their millions—depicting intense gun violence in movies.

It was during this time that I realized the need for this part of the book, something that would answer all the lies about guns that are repeated again and again and often go uncontested. But instead of making up arguments—which would inevitably result in critics saying that no one really makes those claims, or that I misrepresented them—I wanted to use actual quotes. So we started a little project. Each night my staff and I watched countless hours of cable news and read hundreds of newspaper columns and articles. We listened for the quotes about guns and the Second Amendment that seemed to come up most often, the stuff that is so pervasive that it's barely even questioned anymore.

It wasn't difficult. Before long we had enough for not only one book, but several of them. We whittled the quotes down to those that seemed to be repeated the most often—and then we sat down with a team of economists, criminologists, and other gun experts and answered each of them with the truth.

▌ IT'S TIME FOR AMERICA TO HAVE A CONVERSATION ABOUT GUNS. ▌

"Leaders in Washington from both parties and groups like the NRA all say that now is not the time to talk about how gun safety laws can save lives in America. I agree, now is not the time to talk about gun laws. The time for that conversation was long before all those kids in Connecticut died today."

—*REPRESENTATIVE CAROLYN MCCARTHY* (D-NY), *December 14, 2012*

"If there's one thing about the gun debate that everyone seems to agree on, it's that we're going to have a national conversation on the subject. Great news!"

—*CINDY HANDLER* (Huffington Post *columnist*), *January 11, 2013*

Actually, we've had a national conversation about guns for the last two centuries; you just don't like the way it turned out. You may not have noticed, but the so-called gun debate was settled quite a while ago.

In 1791.

▌ WE SHOULD START DRAFTING A BILL TO ENSURE ▌ NEWTOWN NEVER HAPPENS AGAIN.

"[My bill] will ban the sale, the transfer, the importation, and the possession, not retroactively but prospectively. And it will ban the same for big clips, drums, or strips of more than ten bullets. So there will be a bill. We've been working on it now for a year. . . . It'll be ready on the first day."

—*SENATOR DIANNE FEINSTEIN* (D-CA), *December 16, 2012*

Hang on, you've been "working" on this bill for a year? Was it just sitting in a desk drawer waiting for a terrible massacre that you could leverage for political expedience?

Wait—don't answer that.

▌ GUNS ARE LETHAL. ▌

"[T]he point about guns is that they are so much more lethal than anything else you have around. I mean, that is why the American military arms its troops not with knives, but with automatic weapons."
—*NICHOLAS KRISTOF* (New York Times *columnist), January 8, 2013*

"When [a .223-caliber round] hits a human body, the effects are devastating."
—*GENERAL STANLEY MCCHRYSTAL, January 8, 2013*

I know this might be breaking news to Nicholas Kristof, but guns being "more lethal than anything else you have around" is sort of the whole point. The issue should not really be the lethality of the gun, but the psychology of the person holding it. If we are teaching people how to respect their weapons and use them safely, then the times when they're "lethal" are the times when we want them to be.

Outside of hunting and sport shooting, guns serve as "equalizers." With a gun, even an elderly grandmother might well be able to fend off an attacker. Violent criminals are, after all, overwhelmingly young, strong males. To them, anything—from a knife to their bare hand—could easily serve as lethal weapons.

And it is not just Grandma. The equalizer argument applies to most women, to older men, and especially to the disabled—a group that is a particular target for robberies. Guns provide the only effective way for them to defend themselves.

The evidence—and there is plenty of it—points to the exact opposite of what Kristof claims: cutting access to guns mainly disarms law-abiding citizens, making criminals' lives that much easier. Guns allow potential victims to defend themselves when the police aren't there.

Besides, guns may be the most lethal weapon around that's easily accessible, but if we're just talking about overall ability to kill a lot of people, it's hard not to include explosives, which are used by the military and mass killers alike. The first attack on the World Trade Center, in 1993, was a bombing. The Oklahoma City bombing in 1995 killed 168 people and was caused by bombs created from such easily available items as fertilizer (ammonium nitrate), a common cleaning solvent (liquid nitromethane), and diesel fuel. And the worst school massacre in U.S. history, in which thirty-eight people were killed, occurred in 1927 and was carried out with a bomb.

▎NO ONE WANTS TO TAKE YOUR GUNS AWAY. ▎

"No one is saying that people's guns should be taken away, or that taking the Second Amendment rights away. No one is saying that [is the answer] . . ."

—*DON LEMON* (CNN anchor), July 22, 2012

"Nobody questions the Second Amendment's right to bear arms."

—*MAYOR MICHAEL BLOOMBERG* (New York City), December 16, 2012

"Guys, gals, now hear this: No one wants to take away your hunting rifles. No one wants to take away your shotguns. No one wants to take away your revolvers, and no one wants to take away your automatic pistols, as long as said pistols hold no more than ten rounds."

—*STEPHEN KING*, Guns

"I don't want to change the Second Amendment. I don't want to change an American's right to bear an arm in their home to defend people. I want to get rid of these killing machine assault weapons off the street."

—*PIERS MORGAN*, January 7, 2013

> " 'Gun grabber' is a mythical boogeyman. No serious person, including
> Obama, is even proposing taking away owned guns. #StopFearmongering."
>
> —*TOURÉ*, February 16, 2013 (via Twitter)

Anyone who's closely watching the bullying from the control-list crowd, and knows their history, has good reason to be concerned. The environment that's been created is eerily similar to what nations like the United Kingdom, Australia, and Canada experienced just before introducing severe private gun ownership restrictions or banning them altogether.

Here in the United States, the Second Amendment has seemingly gone from being a God-given natural right to a privilege that must be defended. Yet the moment anyone dares voice those concerns they are usually met with mockery and dismissed as a bloodthirsty, paranoid freak who is bitterly clinging to their guns even as the mainstream of society passes them by.

Gun rights advocates are thought by the elite controllists to be creatures with the intelligence of a Neanderthal, stubbornly unwilling to accept "commonsense" gun control measures that would allegedly save the lives of countless American children. The mere mention of a "slippery slope," with the Second Amendment itself being the real target, is brushed off as laughably preposterous conspiracy theory.

The truth—which, as you'll soon see, is not a conspiracy or a theory—is that there are many controllists who want nothing more than to ban guns. They admire Australia and the United Kingdom and Japan and believe that the "civilized" nations of the world have evolved and left America behind. Those countries are the grown-ups while we Americans are the toddlers throwing temper tantrums in a corner.

But controllists have a major problem: the Bill of Rights. Americans have a constitutional right to bear arms—and lots of people want to keep it that way.

According to a December 2012 Gallup poll, 74 percent of Americans oppose a ban on the possession of handguns. So that leaves controllists in a bind: They *believe* that guns have no place among civilians, but they can't really *say* that. So they carefully parse their language. Instead of talking about handgun bans they focus on "military-style" assault weapons or "high-capacity" magazines or laws that make it more difficult to purchase a weapon or ammunition.

But what do you think happens once they get these initial laws passed—do they just stop? Do they pat themselves on the back for getting clips limited to ten bullets, or do they start a new push for eight or five? Do they celebrate getting the sale of new semi-automatics banned, or do they now start to go after all of the ones currently in circulation? That question can easily be answered for anyone willing to listen to what the controllists actually say.

Last we left Senator Dianne Feinstein—the author of the 1994 and 2013 federal assault weapon bans—she was explaining to *60 Minutes* in 1995 that she would've liked to have gotten rid of all so-called assault weapons (not just the specific guns included in the ban), but she just couldn't get it through that pesky Congress:

> If I could've gotten 51 votes in the Senate of the United States for an outright ban, picking up every one of them—Mr. and Mrs. America turn 'em all in—I would have done it.

President Obama and Vice President Joe Biden have also given strong assurances about their commitment to the Second Amendment, but then they put Attorney General Eric Holder in charge of crafting Obama's executive orders on gun control in the wake of the Newtown massacre. Why is that an issue? Because you'd be hard-pressed to find someone more anti-gun (except, of course, when it comes to handing them to Mexican drug cartel members) than Holder.

In a 1995 talk before the Woman's National Democratic Club, Holder said that he hoped we could one day make gun owners feel as ostracized as the smokers who "cower" outside of buildings:

> What we need to do is change the way in which people think about guns, especially young people, and make it something that's not cool, that it's not acceptable, it's not hip to carry a gun anymore, in the way in which we've changed our attitudes about cigarettes. You know, when I was growing up, people smoked all the time. Both my parents did. But over time, we changed the way that people thought about smoking, so now we have people who cower outside of buildings and kind of smoke in private and don't want to admit it.

And later, in the same speech: "We have to be repetitive about this. We need to do this every day of the week, and just *really brainwash people* into thinking about guns in a vastly different way." (emphasis added)

Eric Holder may have been smart enough to not use the word *ban,* but others haven't been so careful.

Remember the quote at the beginning of this section where CNN anchor Don Lemon claimed that "no one is saying" we should take people's guns away? Well, just five months later, he was contradicted by someone he knows very well: Don Lemon.

"We need to get guns and bullets and automatic weapons off the streets," Lemon said. "They should only be available to police officers and to hunt al Qaeda and the Taliban and not hunt elementary school children."

So we should get rid of guns and bullets but no one is saying we should take people's guns away? Same guy. Same year. Incredible.

In case Don Lemon isn't impressed by his own inconsistency, here are a few more concrete examples of people openly calling for gun bans:

How can we possibly have assault weapons? And frankly, why do we need guns? We don't need guns. We have 10,000 murders a year.

—BUZZ BISSINGER, Pulitzer Prize–winning
author and *Daily Beast* columnist

But the logic is faulty, and a close look at it leads to the conclusion that the United States should ban private gun ownership entirely, or almost entirely.

—JEFF MCMAHAN, professor of philosophy at
Rutgers University, writing in the *New York Times*

And this banning mind-set isn't just a reaction to Newtown; it's been around for a while. The editors of the *Los Angeles Times*, in an editorial from 1993 titled "Taming the Monster: Get Rid of the Guns," wrote:

No guns, period, except for those held by law enforcement officials and a few others. . . . Why should America adopt a policy of near-zero tolerance for private gun ownership? Because it's the only alternative to the present insanity. Without both strict limits on access to new weapons and aggressive efforts to reduce the supply of existing weapons, no one can be safer.

Six years later the *Washington Post* got into the act. "No presidential candidate," the paper editorialized, "has yet come out for the most effective proposal to check the terror of gunfire: a ban on the general sale, manufacture and ownership of handguns as well as assault-style weapons."

In other words, the "most effective" plan, according to these editors, is a ban of all handguns and assault weapons. A more recent editorial in the *Economist* seems to agree:

I personally dislike guns. I think the private ownership of guns is a tragic mistake. But a majority of Americans disagree with me, some of them very strongly. And at a certain point, when very large majorities disagree with you, a bit of deference is in order.

. . . I am pretty sure that the sort of gun control that would work—banning all guns—is not going to happen.

Is it possible these opinions don't count because, like corporations, progressives don't consider editorial boards to be "people"?

Back in the present day, Piers Morgan, who claims with a straight face, "I totally respect and admire the Constitution and the Second Amendment and an American's right to defend themselves at home," has also gotten in on the act. This is from his January 10, 2013, show:

> **PIERS MORGAN:** You've got to make a stand somewhere. You have to start somewhere. The logical place to start, given that automatic weapons are banned, is you go to the next level down, semiautomatic weapons. You know, in an ideal world, I'd have all guns gone, as we have in Britain. But this is not my country. And I respect the fact that most Americans wouldn't wear that kind of argument.

Here's a pro tip, Piers, free of charge: when attempting to convince Americans how much you "respect" the Second Amendment, try not to reveal how you would really like to ban all guns. And if you're going to make fun of the slippery slope argument, as you've done so often on your show, maybe try not to use expressions like "You have to start somewhere."

It's important for people to understand where most of these controllists are really coming from. Piers Morgan believes that all guns should be banned. Not just assault weapons or large capacity magazines, but *"all guns gone."* You must listen to everything else he says with that basic framework in mind.

Two days earlier, Morgan had this exchange on his show with Pulitzer Prize–winning *New York Times* columnist Nicholas Kristof:

> **KRISTOF:** So if the only thing that legislators do is reinstitute the assault weapons ban and the high magazine, that will be great. That will be a step forward.
>
> **MORGAN:** But it won't be enough.
>
> **KRISTOF:** But it won't be nearly enough. . . . We have to make a move on handguns as well.

Hey, Touré, do you still think that "no serious person" proposes to take guns away? Still think we should "#StopFearmongering"?

In case you have not heard, Piers Morgan is British. He has seen firsthand how they've successfully been able to change public perception, using one incident at a time to push further and further down the slippery slope that allegedly does not exist. Here's a brief summary of how their gun ban came to be; see if you recognize any similarities to the American debate:

> **1689:** King William of Orange guarantees his subjects (except Catholics) the right to bear arms for self-defense in a new Bill of Rights.
>
> **1819:** In response to civil unrest, a temporary Seizure of Arms Act is passed; it allows constables to search for, and confiscate, arms from people who are "dangerous to the public peace." This expired after two years.
>
> **1870:** A license is needed only if you want to carry a firearm outside of your home.

1903: The Pistols Act is introduced and seems to be full of common sense. No guns for drunks or the mentally insane, and licenses are required for handgun purchases.

1920: The Firearms Act ushers in the first registration system and gives police the power to deny a license to anyone "unfitted to be trusted with a firearm." According to historian Clayton Cramer, this is the first true pivot point for the United Kingdom, as "the ownership of firearms ceased to be a right of Englishmen, and instead became a privilege."

1937: An update to the Firearm Act is passed that raises the minimum age to buy a gun, gives police more power to regulate licenses, and bans most fully automatic weapons. The home secretary also rules that self-defense is no longer a valid reason to be granted a gun certificate.

1967: The Criminal Justice Act expands licensing to shotguns.

1968: Existing gun laws are placed into a single statute. Applicants have to show good reason for carrying ammunition and guns. The Home Office is also given the power to set fees for shotgun licenses.

1988: After the Hungerford Massacre, in which a crazy person uses two semi-automatic rifles to kill fifteen people, an amendment to the Firearms Act is passed. According to the BBC, this amendment "banned semi-automatic and pump-action rifles; weapons which fire explosive ammunition; short shotguns with magazines; and elevated pump-action and self-loading rifles. Registration was also made mandatory for shotguns, which were required to be kept in secure storage."

1997: After the Dunblane massacre results in the deaths of sixteen children and a teacher (the killer uses two pistols and two revolvers), another Firearms Act amendment is passed, this one essentially banning all handguns.

2006: After a series of gun-related homicides get national attention, the Violent Crime Reduction Act is passed, making it a crime to make or sell imitation guns and further restricting the use of "air weapons."

If that does not prove how the slippery slope—from Bill of Rights to total ban actually works—then I don't know what does. So, you'll have to excuse us, Piers, when we get a little dodgy about your assault weapon ban proposal or when CNN anchors and major newspaper columnists advocate for "zero tolerance" on private gun ownership.

We've seen this movie before and we know how it ends.

▌ WELL, CAN'T WE AT LEAST CLARIFY THE SECOND AMENDMENT? ▌

"Is there an argument for the Second Amendment to be
repealed and to be clarified and be redrafted?"
—*PIERS MORGAN*, December 18, 2012

I know that Piers isn't an American citizen, so I'll give him the benefit of the doubt and assume he doesn't quite understand how this works in the United States.

Yes, Piers, the Second Amendment could be repealed, clarified, or redrafted. And you could lead all of cable news in ratings. Both of those things are *technically* possible—but neither will ever happen.

The Constitution is, of course, not immutable. When the American people wish to change the Constitution, they can do so through the amendment process detailed in Article V. In fact, the people themselves (acting through their state legislatures) can use Article V to call a convention to propose a particular amendment, or they can call a convention to propose an entirely new constitution.

Yet, for well over two centuries, through wars and peace, mob violence, gang violence, and unthinkable public massacres, no serious attempt has ever been made to repeal or redraft the Second

Amendment. If one had been, it's doubtful that even a single state would've ratified the proposal. Even today, with what the media alleges is a completely changed national attitude toward guns, it is very likely that a proposal to repeal the Second Amendment would be ratified by a grand total of zero states.

However, plenty of states have gone the other way, amending their state constitutions toward a clearer understanding of the right to keep and bear arms being an individual right. The most recent example is Louisiana, where nearly 73 percent of voters in 2012 approved an amendment to the state constitution making it much more difficult for gun control legislation to pass.

The old Louisiana constitution read:

> The right of each citizen to keep and bear arms shall not be abridged, but this provision shall not prevent the passage of laws to prohibit the carrying of weapons concealed on the person.

But this was replaced with far stronger wording:

> The right of each citizen to acquire, keep, possess, transport, carry, transfer, and use arms for defense of life and liberty, and for all other legitimate purposes is fundamental and shall not be denied or infringed, and any restriction on this right shall be subject to strict scrutiny.

So, yes, Piers—we could definitely clarify all of this for you—but probably not in the direction you think.

**▍THAT MAY BE, BUT EVEN THOMAS JEFFERSON ▍
WANTED THE SECOND AMENDMENT TO EXPIRE.**

"Thomas Jefferson, who wrote the Second Amendment, said that it should be revisited every 20 years to see if it is still appropriate."
—*CHRISTOPHER KENNEDY LAWFORD*, January 7, 2013

A small point of clarification for Mr. Lawford: Thomas Jefferson didn't write the Second Amendment. In fact, he was not even in the country at the time it was created; he was the United States minister plenipotentiary to France. It was James Madison who took the numerous suggestions for the language of the Second Amendment and synthesized them into a proposal that Congress subsequently debated, amended, and sent to the states for ratification.

But let's excuse for a second the fact that JFK's nephew—a man who is a self-described "author, activist and actor" and who routinely puts himself on television to discuss gun control—does not even know who actually wrote the Second Amendment. He's still wrong. Jefferson never said that the Second Amendment in particular ought to be reexamined every twenty years. What he *did* say one time in a letter to Madison—and what I assume Lawford was referring to—was that *all* laws, including the U.S. Constitution, ought to automatically expire after twenty years:

On similar ground it may be proved that no society can make a perpetual constitution, or even a perpetual law. The earth belongs to the living generation. They may manage it then, and what proceeds from it, as they please, during their usufruct. They are masters too of their own persons, and consequently may govern them as they please. But persons and property make the sum of the objects of government. The constitution and the laws of their predecessors extinguished them, in their natural course, with those whose will gave them being. This could preserve that being till it ceased to be itself, and no longer. Every constitution, then, and every law, naturally expires at the end of 19 years. If it be enforced longer, it is an act of force and not of right.

—LETTER FROM THOMAS JEFFERSON, in
Paris, to James Madison, September 6, 1789

While this letter makes Jefferson sound as though he could be a member of the Center for American Progress, there's actually an important lesson here: Jefferson lost. His views were in the extreme minority. Most Americans, including James Madison, hoped that the new Constitution of 1787 would provide long-term stability to the United States.

And that's exactly what has happened.

Since the Constitution is not a "living" document, it has guaranteed generations of Americans that the bedrock principles of freedom will endure.

But Lawford is wrong for another reason as well. By focusing on this one letter, he's missing a much larger point: even if laws were reviewed, Jefferson would have always insisted that any new constitution respect the natural rights of mankind. As he affirmed in his writings, including the Declaration of Independence, the essential purpose of government is to protect our God-given rights.

Whether a law was to expire in ten years, twenty years, or one hundred years is irrelevant—Jefferson would always be against any effort to suppress our inalienable rights. Like the other Founders, Jefferson believed there were many different ways in which a government could be structured, but that every legitimate government must protect—and never violate—the natural rights of mankind.

Finally, if Lawford is really so supportive of Jefferson's idea, then he also must be willing to throw out every major current gun control law that is more than twenty years old. That would wipe out the vast majority of federal gun control laws—including the National Firearms Act of 1934 and the Gun Control Act of 1968. Most state gun control laws would disappear as well. The result? The United States of 2013 would look a lot like the United States of 1788—a nation with no constitutional guarantee about the right to bear arms, but also a nation with a lot of guns and almost no laws restricting them.

▌THE UNITED STATES HAS THE HIGHEST GUN ▌
MURDER RATE IN THE DEVELOPED WORLD.

"You have by far the worst rate of gun murder and gun crime
of any of the civilized countries of this world. . . ."

—PIERS MORGAN, December 18, 2012

This all sounds pretty plausible—which is probably why this line is repeated so often. Yet things are a lot more complicated than they seem.

It's not clear exactly what countries Morgan has picked when he says other "civilized" countries, but it is possible to generate almost any kind of result by picking the "right" set of countries.

First, let's just be clear that lots of nations, including "civilized" ones, suffer from higher overall murder and gun murder rates than America. In 2011, the U.S. murder rate was 4.7 per 100,000 people and the gun murder rate was 3.2. Much of Eastern Europe, most of Southeast Asia, the Caribbean, Africa, all but one South American nation, and all of Central America and Mexico suffer from higher murder rates than we do. For example, despite very strict gun control, homicide rates in Russia and Brazil have averaged about four to five times higher than ours over the last decade. As the *Washington Post* reported:

> The dubious distinction of having the most gun violence goes to Honduras, at 68.43 homicides by firearm per 100,000 people, even though it only has 6.2 firearms per 100 people. Other parts of South America and South Africa also rank highly, while the United States is somewhere near the mid-range.

In fact, if you look across all nations and not just a select few, what you find is that those with the strictest gun control laws also tend to have the highest murder rates. Gun control advocates prefer to use the very questionable data from the pro-gun control "Small Arms Survey" to make their case—but even that data proves that higher rates of gun ownership correlate with fewer deaths. (See charts.)

More Guns, More Murder?

Developed Countries
(Other Than the U.S.)

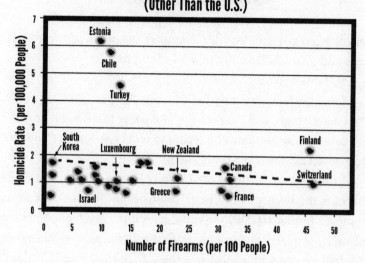

Homicide Rate (per 100,000 People)

Estonia
Chile
Turkey
South Korea
Luxembourg
New Zealand
Finland
Canada
Switzerland
Israel
Greece
France

Number of Firearms (per 100 People)

All Other Countries

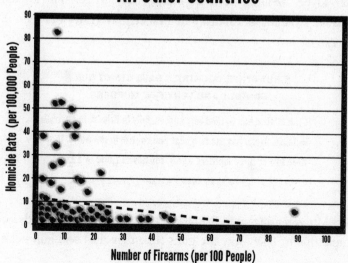

Homicide Rate (per 100,000 People)

Number of Firearms (per 100 People)

▌ OKAY, BUT THE OVERALL U.S. MURDER RATE IS MUCH ▌ HIGHER THAN OTHER WEALTHY COUNTRIES'.

"[T]he American murder rate is roughly 15 times that of other wealthy countries, which have much tougher laws controlling private ownership of guns."

—NEW YORK TIMES *(editorial), December 17, 2012*

Oh, okay, so now it's "wealthy" countries instead of just "civilized" ones and it's *overall* murder instead of gun murder.

Still totally wrong.

The U.S. homicide rate in 2011 was 4.7 per 100,000 people. That is very high, and I'm certainly not going to defend it or make the case that we shouldn't be trying to reduce it—but it's *nowhere near* what the *New York Times* claims.

I took a look through the United Nations data on homicide rates for the twenty "wealthiest" countries in the world by gross domestic product (GDP). As you'd expect, the per capita rates are all over the place, but in only one case (Singapore—where they still lash people with canes) was the U.S. murder rate "15 times" higher. Most of the countries that reasonable people would consider to be "wealthy" *and* "civilized," like Switzerland, Sweden, Canada, Finland, Germany, and France, have rates between 0.7 and 2.5.

▌ BUT OTHER COUNTRIES HAVE STRICT GUN ▌ CONTROL AND VERY FEW MURDERS.

"[G]un control has worked very successfully in Britain, in Australia, in Japan. Japan has the toughest gun control in the world. They have two or three murders a year. You have 11,000 to 12,000."

—*PIERS MORGAN, December 17, 2012*

Piers Morgan grew up in Britain, so he thinks he understands how simple this is: take away the guns (like they did) and gun deaths go away. But that is way too simplistic. You have to look systemati-cally across time and across as many countries as possible if you care about making a fair comparison and finding the truth—not just helping your political agenda.

The United Kingdom has enjoyed very low overall crime rates for a long time—since long before Piers Morgan was even born, back in the days when gun ownership was much more widespread. In fact, murder and armed robberies were almost nonexistent. It might sound unbelievable, but back in 1904, London—a city with a population of around 7 million and the envy of the civilized world—reported just two gun murders and five armed robberies.

Crime differs across nations and over time for a vast array of reasons, some of which we may never fully understand. However, for countries that have abruptly changed their rules regarding gun ownership or gun carrying, we can look at what happened right after the changes.

And what do we find? The results might surprise you: *In every single place that all guns or handguns were banned, murder rates went up.*

Let's take another look at Great Britain first—a place where guns have never been as freely available as they have been in the United States.

We previously looked at the overall gun control time line, but now let's zero in on a few key parts. According to Joyce Lee Malcolm, a professor at George Mason University Law School and author of *Guns and Violence: The English Experience,* "Since 1920, anyone in Britain wanting a handgun had to obtain a certificate from his local police stating he was fit to own a weapon and had good reason to have one. Over the years, the definition of 'good reason' gradually narrowed. By 1969, self-defense was never a good reason for a permit."

In 1987, after a massacre in Hungerford, England, killed sixteen people and wounded fourteen others (since no one else had a gun, including the police, the killer roamed for eight hours), the government cracked down. Semi-automatic rifles were banned and shotguns were regulated like handguns.

Nine years later, the Dunblane massacre in Scotland resulted in the final blow to gun ownership. The Firearms Act of 1997 banned handguns almost entirely—forcing lawful owners to turn them in or face ten years in prison.

What happened next? Professor Malcolm has summarized it well:

> The results have not been what proponents of the act wanted. Within a decade of the handgun ban and the confiscation of handguns from registered owners, crime with handguns had doubled according to British government crime reports. Gun crime, not a serious problem in the past, now is. Armed street gangs have some British police carrying guns for the first time. Moreover, another massacre occurred in June 2010. Derrick Bird, a taxi driver in Cumbria, shot his brother and a colleague then drove off through rural villages killing 12 people and injuring 11 more before killing himself.

The homicide rate in Britain rose dramatically for seven years after the ban, from 1.1 homicides per 100,000 people in 1996 to 1.8 in 2003. At that point, fed up with the sudden increase in murder and violent crime, the police force was expanded by 16 percent between 2001 and 2005. Unsurprisingly, more police meant less crime. Still, even with the increased police presence, crime generally remained higher than before the Firearms Act.

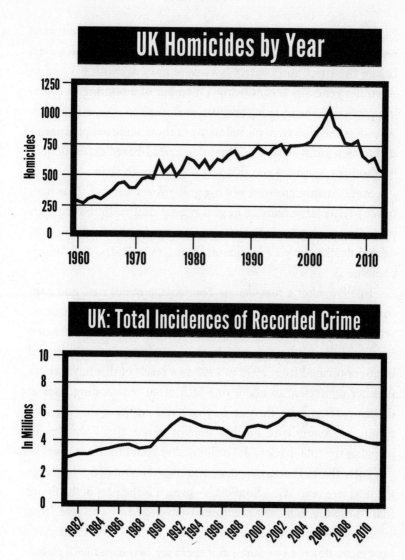

Australia was Morgan's second example, and the numbers there paint an even less convincing picture, especially when you study how certain crime rates changed after their gun ban.

But, before we get to the stats, a quick primer on Australia is in order. Unlike the United States, Australia does not have a Bill of

Rights or a constitutional guarantee to bear arms. As a result, guns were never really a big part of the Australian culture. In fact, even before the strict gun control laws were passed, owning a gun in Australia generally meant being a member of a hunting or sporting group, or showing an occupational need to own a handgun. And after the laws were passed many of these same people continued to own guns—either by obtaining a need-based exemption, or by choosing a style of gun that was not part of the ban.

Since Australians were not big gun owners anyway, there have never been a large number of gun-related deaths. In the six years preceding the buyback, the country averaged only about 550 gun-related deaths per year (accidents, murders, suicides, and "other" combined).

In 1996, after a massacre is Tasmania, a major new gun control effort began across Australia. This consisted of new bans on semi-automatic weapons along with a major buyback of existing (and now illegal) firearms. More than 650,000 guns were turned in or confiscated from 1996 to 1997 as a result of this buyback—a number equivalent to about one-fifth of all outstanding guns at the time. (Ironically, the gun buyback did not have the intended result, as Australians quickly bought more single-shot guns, bringing the total back to 3.2 million after about fourteen years.)

After the buyback, gun-deaths averaged about 356 a year over the next five years. Gun homicides—which is the part of the figure that Morgan specifically mentioned—averaged 82 per year from 1991 to 1996, and 58 per year from 1997 to 2001. Did those averages move down a bit? Sure—but there are two issues with claiming a win based on that: first, the overall numbers are so small that the change is statistically irrelevant, and second, people have found ways to kill that don't involve a gun.

If instead of looking only at gun-related homicides you look at the *overall* number of homicides before and after the ban, you find that there's not a lot of difference. Non-gun homicides averaged about 240 per year from 1991 to 1996 and increased to about 255 per year from 1997 to 2001. Does that mean that the gun control laws forced more people to become killers? No, of course not, but it very well may mean that those who would've used a gun instead use something else, like a knife.

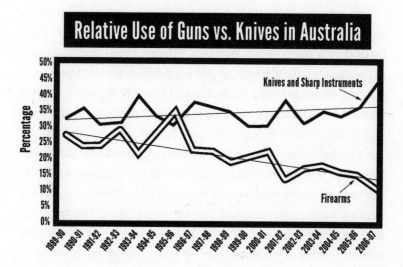

Relative Use of Guns vs. Knives in Australia

According to Piers Morgan's assumption, overall murder rates should have initially plummeted after the gun buyback and then risen back up over time as Australians replenished their guns. But that simply did not happen. Instead, total homicides have basically remained at the same very low rate they were at since before the buyback.

Several major studies that have researched the buyback have reached similar conclusions. One, done by Wang-Sheng Lee and Sandy Suardi of the Melbourne Institute of Applied Economic and Social Research, at the University of Melbourne, concluded that the "results of these tests suggest that the NFA [the 1996–97 National Firearms Agreement] did not have any large effects on reducing firearm homicide or suicide rates."

A second study, done by Jeanine Baker of the Sporting

Shooters Association of Australia and Samara McPhedran of the University of Sydney, and published in the *British Journal of Criminology*, reached a similar conclusion: "Homicide patterns (firearm and non-firearm) were not influenced by the NFA, the conclusion being that the gun buy-back and restrictive legislative changes had no influence on firearm homicide in Australia."

One final note on the agreement's impact on Australian crime. Armed robberies exploded after the new laws, from about 6,000 in 1996 to around 10,000 between 1998 and 2001, before declining to pre-buyback levels in 2004. In other words, fewer guns resulted in more armed robberies and roughly the same number of murders—not exactly a shining example of the utopian society that awaits all of us if only we'd agree to ban semi-automatics.

Finally, Japan—a nation that, unlike Australia and the United Kingdom, has not experienced any sudden changes in gun policies and is therefore more difficult to fairly evaluate. Japan has imposed strict gun control for centuries, long before crime data began to be systematically collected. Guns are allowed for hunting—there were more than 400,000 registered firearms in 2011—but handguns are banned.

Control enthusiasts love to point to Japan, which has a very low murder rate, as the prime example of how fewer guns equates to less crime and far fewer homicides. But if that theory were true, then it should always be true. And it's simply not.

Take Switzerland, for example. As I mentioned earlier, Switzerland has the third-highest rate of firearms per capita in the world. So, it stands to reason, then, that Switzerland's streets must be flowing in blood, right?

Not even close.

Switzerland had a gun homicide rate of 0.5 per 100,000 people in 2010. Their overall homicide rate was 0.7, ranking the country well below other gun control havens like Australia (1.0), the United Kingdom (1.2), and Canada (1.6).

This theory falls apart when you look at it from the other side as well. The Netherlands, for example, has one of the lowest rates of gun ownership in Europe at 3.9 per capita, but its homicide rate (1.1) is nowhere near the bottom. Switzerland, Austria, Germany, Italy, Spain, Norway, and Sweden all have lower murder rates than the Netherlands—and far more guns per capita.

It's easy to cherry-pick data or point to one country and say that it proves a theory—it's much harder, but far more worthwhile, to look across entire sets of data and see whether that theory holds up. In this case, it simply doesn't.

Americans have seen this same pattern play out here at home in cities like Washington, D.C., and Chicago and in states like Massachusetts—all of which have implemented very tough gun control laws or outright bans.

D.C.'s handgun ban (which also mandated that other firearms, including rifles and shotguns, be kept unloaded and disassembled) went into effect in early 1977. Since then, there has been only one year (1985) when that city's murder rate fell below what it was in the year before the ban. If this were a general, nationwide trend, then we should see the murder rate in other cities also increase during that time. But that's not what happened. In the twenty-nine years of data we have since the ban, D.C.'s murder rate ranked in the top four among the fifty largest U.S. cities in 19 of those years. In 15 of those 19 years D.C. ranked either first or second in the country. Prior to the ban, D.C. was never ranked that high. They ranked in the top fifteen just once.

Was there something special about D.C. that kept the ban from working? Probably not, since we often see this same trend play out in other cities with restrictive gun control. Before Chicago's ban in 1982, its murder rate per 100,000 people, which was falling from 27 to 22 in the prior five years, suddenly stopped falling and instead rose slightly to 23 in the five years afterward. Tracing that change directly to the handgun ban is, of course, impossible, but it's pretty stunning when you look at what happened in the counties surrounding the city of Chicago over this same time. According to John Lott, "Chicago's murder rate fell from being 8.1 times greater than its neighbors in 1977 to 5.5 times in 1982, and then went way up to 12 times greater in 1987."

And Massachusetts, which passed laws in 1998 aimed at making it very difficult to own a gun (and banning semi-automatic "assault weapons" outright), has experienced the same kind of results. While the laws did work to make it difficult for law-abiding people to own guns (there were 1.5 million active licenses in 1998 and only 200,000 four years later), it had no effect on people who generally ignore laws anyway. Those people are sometimes referred to as "criminals."

According to a February, 2013 article in the *Boston Globe*, "Murders committed with firearms *have increased significantly*, aggravated assaults and robberies involving guns *have risen*, and gunshot injuries *are up*, according to FBI and state data." (emphasis added)

In 2011, Massachusetts had 122 firearm homicides. This was, according to the *Globe*, "a striking increase from the 65 in 1998." Other categories of violent crime—from aggravated assault (up 26.7 percent) to armed robbery (up 20.7 percent)—also increased.

Of course, gun control advocates claim that none of these locations was a fair test for gun bans or extremely strict regulations. They say that, unless guns are banned across the entire country, criminals in one location can simply drive to another to obtain them. But if that's true, then in a worst-case scenario, you might expect homicide and violent crime rates to continue on whatever trend they were already on. In other words, if the ban simply doesn't work, then it should have no impact and each location's homicide and crime rate should continue at whatever pace it was on relative to the locations around it that did not implement bans.

But that's not what happened. In Massachusetts, for example, the state's lowest per capita homicide rate occurred in 1997, the year before the ban. By 2011 it had increased by 47 percent, bucking the national trend, which was down. Nationwide, the homicide rate over that same time period was *down* 31 percent.

And you can't blame a regional quirk, either. The year the ban took place Massachusetts had a murder rate that was roughly 70 percent of other states in the Northeast (New York, Connecticut, Rhode Island, Maine, Vermont, New Hampshire). But now? Homicides in Massachusetts are 125 percent of the average of those other states.

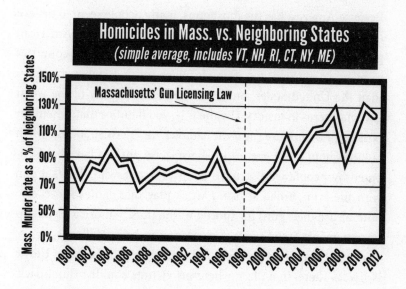

If all of this data doesn't do it for you, then there's another response to those who say that none of these bans are good tests, a response that is more about common sense than studies and stats: if those who proposed these bans *expected* violent crime rates to increase, why didn't they warn us in advance?

▌ THE UNITED STATES IS UNIQUE IN SUFFERING FROM GUN MASSACRES. ▌

"[I]t's so unbelievable. And it only happens in America. And it happens
again and again. There was another shooting yesterday. Three people killed,
I think in a hospital. We kill people in schools. We kill them in hospitals.
We kill them in religious organizations. We kill them when they're young.
We kill them when they're old. And we've just got to stop this."

—*MAYOR MICHAEL BLOOMBERG, December 22, 2012*

"No other country in the world has the problem
that America has with gun massacres."

—*RACHEL MADDOW, January 11, 2011*

Because America has the most guns, many people seem to believe
that multiple-victim public massacres are an exclusively American
phenomenon. But that's simply not the case. Most of the countries
in Western Europe, for example, have much tougher gun laws
than the United States, but have experienced many of the worst
gun massacres in history. (By the way, you'll notice that, whenever
possible, I do not use the term "shooter" or "mass shooting" when
talking about these events. I believe those phrases have been co-
opted by people who want to paint everyone who shoots a gun
with the same broad stroke. I won't play that game. Those who
hunt or use their guns for sport are "shooters"—those who kill innocent people with them are murderers and glory killers.)

In 2011, a thirty-two-year-old man visited the island of Utoya,
Norway. There, in a place where his victims couldn't shoot back,
he murdered 69 people and injured at least 110. This remains the
worst massacre ever committed by a single person. In Mumbai,
India, on November 26, 2008, 164 people were killed and another
308 wounded when terrorists wielding machine guns and gre-
nades invaded hotels, a train station, and a Jewish cultural center.
Both of those massacres eclipsed anything that has occurred in
the United States.

Up until the attack in Newtown, Connecticut, the three worst K–12 public school massacres in the world had all occurred in Europe. The worst occurred in 2002 in a high school in Erfurt, Germany, when eighteen were killed. The second-worst was the Dunblane massacre in Scotland, in which sixteen kindergartners and their teacher were killed. The third-worst, with fifteen dead, happened in Winnenden, Germany. (By the way, most of the mass murderers I reference did what they did to be famous. I refuse to give them that satisfaction and will not mention their names in this book.)

When guns aren't as easily available, psychopaths often turn to other weapons. In 2009, a twenty-year-old man armed with a knife and a hatchet attacked a day-care center in Belgium, where he hacked and stabbed two adults and thirteen babies. Two nine-month-old babies and one day-care worker were killed. Media reports state that the killer dyed his hair red and was obsessed with the Batman movie *The Dark Knight*. He committed the massacre on the one-year anniversary of the death of Heath Ledger, the actor who played the Joker in that movie.

In 2008, a thirty-seven-year-old man entered an elementary school in Osaka, Japan, armed with a kitchen knife. He murdered eight children and seriously wounded thirteen other kids, along with two teachers.

Throughout the three-year period 2010–2012, a series of attacks on elementary schools and day-care centers were committed in the People's Republic of China using knives, cleavers, hammers, axes, and box-cutters. China has suppressed and censored much of the news about these attacks—partially to prevent copycat crimes, and partially to protect themselves from intense national horror and embarrassment—but here are a few that we do know of:

2010

—A forty-one-year-old man stabbed an unknown number of
    students in an elementary school. Eight were reported to be killed.

—A thirty-three-year-old man stabbed sixteen students and a teacher in an elementary school. Death toll unknown.

—A forty-seven-year-old man stabbed twenty-eight students, two teachers, and one security guard in a kindergarten. Most of the students were four years old. Death toll unknown.

—A man (age unknown) armed with a hammer attacked children in a preschool. He then committed suicide by dousing himself in gasoline and setting himself on fire. The number of injured and killed is unknown.

—A forty-eight-year-old man, armed with a cleaver, attacked a kindergarten class, where he murdered seven children and two adults and injured eleven others.

—A twenty-six-year-old man slashed more than twenty children and staff at a kindergarten, killing three children and one teacher.

2011

—An employee at a child-care center (age unknown), armed with a box-cutter, slashed eight children, all aged four or five. Death toll unknown.

—A thirty-year-old man, armed with an axe, murdered a one-year-old and a four-year-old and four adults who where taking their children to a nursery school.

2012

—A thirty-six-year-old man hacked and stabbed an elderly woman and twenty-three children at an elementary school. It was reported that, due to immediate trauma care in three different hospitals, none of the victims died, although some were seriously injured, with fingers and ears cut off.

—A seventeen-year-old man stabbed to death nine people and wounded four others with a knife in China's Liaoning Province following an argument with his girlfriend.

Mass murders happen with appalling regularity in Mexico, a place with restrictive gun control laws. In 2010, Juárez, Mexico, experienced at least two gun-related mass killings—one in February when thirteen people were killed at a party, and another in September, when eight were killed inside a bar. (Juárez is right across the Rio Grande from El Paso, Texas, which was recently named the "safest large city in America.") Obviously, many of these massacres in Mexico are related to drug cartels, but it's strange how they occur so frequently in places that have adopted restrictive gun controls. It's almost as though cartel or gang members don't care about the law.

John Lott, an economist and researcher who has performed some of the most comprehensive research to date about the impact of guns on crime (Lott also helped me immensely with research for this book), has put together a partial list of gun-related mass homicides in Europe since 2001 (see link below), and it's pretty exhausting to read. You quickly realize that, while those attacks don't make headlines over here, they are just as heartbreaking and confusing. You also soon realize something else: all of the multiple-victim public massacres in Western Europe, as well as all of those in the United States where at least three people died, have occurred in places where civilians cannot legally bring guns.

For a partial list of cases to show that "it only happens in America" is false see: http://fxn.ws/ZXBTRa.

▌ THEN WHY ARE GUN MASSACRES NOW HAPPENING ▌ MORE THAN EVER HERE IN THE UNITED STATES?

"These shootings are becoming all too common, and it's too easy for dangerous people to get the weapons that help them perform mass executions like today's."
—*REPRESENTATIVE CAROLYN MCCARTHY* (D-NY), December 14, 2012

"Mass shootings are not a new phenomenon in our country. But if it seems like the worst of them are happening more frequently these days, it's because that's true."
—*RACHEL MADDOW*, December 17, 2012

Actually, no, Rachel, that's not true. Gun massacres are *not* becoming more common. There is a *perception* that we have a sudden crisis (just as there is a perception that a lot of people watch your show), but perception does not equal reality.

Some of this is human nature. Massacres like the ones in Aurora and Newtown are incomprehensible to most people. Our sense of grief and loss and guilt is so overwhelming—and the media coverage so unending—that our perception of the event is demonstrably altered; the details are seared into our minds. We may not remember much about a gang killing in Chicago or a robbery in Cleveland, but we damn well remember the look on those kids' faces as they ran out of Columbine.

The massacres that most of us hear about and react to—the Columbines, Virginia Techs, Auroras, and Newtowns of the world—are extremely uncommon events. The left-wing magazine *Mother Jones,* whose data, as you'll soon see, is extremely suspect, counted sixty-two gun-related mass homicides over the last thirty years, and reported that a total of 513 people have been killed in these attacks. For comparison purposes—solely to show the rarity of these massacres—3,696 people were killed in the United States by lightning over the forty-four-year period from 1959 to 2003.

That comparison is not at all meant to diminish any of the victims. It's simply meant to show why Congresswoman McCarthy is so wrong when she uses the word *common* in the same sentence that she mentions "mass executions." It's simply not true.

It is true, however, that mass killings do sometimes appear in clusters. This might just be sheer randomness (airline accidents also have a tendency to feel this way), but it's likely also due to some copycat effect. The killer from Newtown, for example, was reportedly "motivated by . . . a strong desire to kill more people than another infamous mass murderer. . . . [He] saw himself as being in direct competition with . . . a Norwegian man who killed 77 people in July 2011."

To separate fact from perception, let's take a closer look at mass murders that involve guns. First, we've got to define exactly what we are assessing: *all* gun-related mass killings, or just those *in public places* (the type that usually make headlines and capture the public's attention).

James Alan Fox, a criminologist at Northeastern University who is an expert on these incidents, recently noted the following:

> What is abundantly clear from the full array of mass shootings, besides the lack of any trend upward or downward, is the largely random variability in the annual counts. There have been several points in time when journalists and other people have speculated about a possible epidemic in response to a flurry of high-profile shootings. Yet these speculations have always proven to be incorrect when subsequent years reveal more moderate levels.

In case people thought that was a little murky, Fox summed up the FBI and police data he'd used to reach his conclusion like this: "[M]ass shootings have not increased in number or in overall body count, at least not over the past several decades."

Other experts agree. John Lott focuses on gun-related mass killings that take place in public places, excluding attacks involving gangs. Lott reports that, from 1977 to 2010, there is even a slight decline in these types of killings. Similarly, Grant Duwe, author of *Mass Murder in the United States: A History,* points to a decline in overall public mass murders, dropping from 43 total cases in the 1990s to 26 in the first decade of the twenty-first century. Even the National Institute of Justice agrees that these incidents are simply not a large enough part of the problem to merit the attention we put on stopping them. Their review of the data yielded an even smaller annual fatality number than other experts:

> Fatalities from mass shootings (those with 4 or more victims in a particular place and time) account on average for 35 fatalities per year. Policies that address the larger firearm homicide issue will have a far greater impact even if they do not address the particular issues of mass shootings.

Rachel Maddow, along with most of the others who claim that mass killings are on the rise, never bother to look into the facts. Instead they rely on reports like the one done by *Mother Jones* (which called mass killings an "epidemic"), without questioning their methodology. But that's a big mistake, because the *Mother Jones* report does not stand up to any kind of scrutiny, let alone academic standards. For example, the first criterion listed by *Mother Jones* is:

> The killings were carried out by a lone shooter. (Except in the case of the Columbine massacre and the Westside Middle School killings, both of which involved two shooters.)

Now, let me reword that into what they really meant to say:

> The killings were carried about by a lone shooter. (Except in the case of two school shootings that we randomly included because there was no way we could ever leave Columbine out.)

As Professor Fox pointed out, other important criteria in their approach are also "hard to defend" or "not necessarily applied consistently." For example:

Mother Jones included the 1993 Chuck E. Cheese robbery/ massacre of four people committed by a former employee, but excluded the Brown's Chicken robbery/massacre of seven victims that occurred the very same year, presumably because two perpetrators were involved in the latter incident or perhaps because these gunmen had no prior connection to the restaurant.

The *Mother Jones* methodology was created to ensure that only a very specific set of killings would be generated—a set that fit their narrative about an "epidemic" of these type of crimes. So what happens when you look at the data far more broadly and take into account *all* gun-related mass killings (four or more victims, not including the gunman) that were reported to the FBI by local law enforcement?

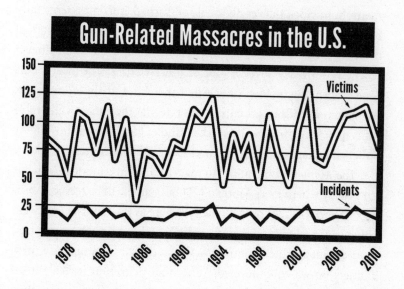

Paints a slightly different picture, doesn't it? Maybe that's why *Mother Jones,* and those who follow its lead—chose to ignore it.

▍ NO MASS KILLINGS HAVE EVER BEEN STOPPED ▍ BY SOMEONE ELSE WITH A GUN.

"In the last 30 years there have been 62 mass shootings. Not a single one has ever been thwarted by a civilian despite America being a heavily armed country."

—PIERS MORGAN, January 9, 2013

If you take this quote at face value it's so stupid that it almost doesn't deserve a response. Of course none of the "mass shootings" were stopped—if they'd been stopped they wouldn't be called "mass shootings." It's like saying that not a single one of the 32,367 traffic fatalities that occurred in 2011 was thwarted by seat belts or air bags or speed limits. Yeah—no kidding, that's why they're fatalities.

What Morgan's circular argument leaves out is the fact that many homicides that easily could've turned into massacres *have* been stopped by others with a gun. You don't hear much about these incidents because they either never happened or they never reached the "mass" level of four or more victims. The local media might cover the incident, but when there's no grisly crime scene, no shaken friends or parents to interview at their most vulnerable time, no feeding frenzy about what kind of gun it was or how many bullets the magazine held, the national media loses interest fast.

The *Mother Jones* "guide" to mass killings in America (which is very likely where Piers Morgan gets his statistic of "62 mass shootings" from) includes only incidents where at least four people were killed (not including the gunman) in one location. This definition ensures that any incident used in the study is, by definition, a mass killing that was not stopped. What that definition leaves out, of course, are all the times when someone was stopped before they could kill anyone, or after killing fewer than four people. If you don't think that has ever happened, keep reading.

On April 20, 1999, the country sat stunned as the Columbine massacre unfolded right in front of our eyes. Most people remember exactly where they were when it happened—it was a "JFK assassination" moment for a new generation.

But I guarantee that almost no one remembers where they were nearly eighteen months earlier, on October 1, 1997.

On that day a sixteen-year-old boy slit his mother's throat, grabbed her rifle, put on a trench coat, and left for Pearl High School in Pearl, Mississippi. When he arrived he headed for the courtyard and began to fire, hitting nine of his fellow students and killing two.

Police say that the killer's plan was to leave the high school and drive to nearby Pearl Junior High School to start shooting again. But as the boy left the school and began to drive his car through the parking lot he was confronted by a Colt .45 pointed through the windshield. Stunned, the boy crashed his car. The man with the gun, Vice Principal Joel Myrick, held it to the boy's head, point-blank. "Why are you shooting my kids?" he asked him.

Myrick, who'd run to his truck to retrieve his gun as soon as he'd heard the shooting start, held the killer at gunpoint until police arrived. The boy was later found to have thirty-six rounds still in his pockets.

No one knows how many lives were saved by preventing the boy from making it to the other school, and no one knows whether the two kids who were killed could've been saved had Myrick's gun been closer. But we do know that this incident never reached "mass" status and therefore never captured the attention of the media, the public, *Mother Jones,* or Piers Morgan.

Ten years later, on Sunday, December 9, 2007, a twenty-four-year-old man showed up at the Christian "Youth with a Mission" training center in the Denver suburbs and murdered two teenagers. He then drove south to Colorado Springs, site of the New Life megachurch. Like a movie theater, the church was densely packed with a huge crowd of people.

In the parking lot he immediately opened fire, killing two teenage sisters. Then, armed with a rifle, two semi-automatic handguns, and a thousand rounds of ammunition, he entered the church. In a Web post found after the incident, the killer had written, "All I want to do is kill and injure as many of you [Christians] . . . as I can."

But that was not going to happen. Someone was ready for him.

Jeanne Assam, a volunteer security guard for the church, was carrying a licensed handgun and quickly confronted the gunman. When he didn't comply she shot him several times until he went down. He then shot himself in the head, putting an end to the attack. According to Pastor Brady Boyd, "she probably saved over 100 lives."

But the New Life Church and Pearl, Mississippi, mass-killings-that-weren't are not the only ones ignored by people like Piers Morgan, who desperately want people to believe that guns have never stopped a would-be mass killer.

In 1998, a fourteen-year-old boy took his father's .25-caliber handgun and brought it to a Friday night junior high school dance at a local banquet hall in Edinboro, Pennsylvania. On the restaurant patio, he shot a science teacher in the head, killing him. Next, the killer went into the hall and fired several shots, wounding two students. The restaurant's owner, James Strand, grabbed his shotgun, followed the boy out, and persuaded him to surrender. Strand held the boy for another ten minutes until the police arrived.

In 1991, at a Shoney's restaurant in Anniston, Alabama, two criminals using stolen handguns herded twenty customers and employees into the walk-in refrigerator. Holding the manager at gunpoint, the two men began to rob the restaurant, but they failed to notice another customer, Thomas Glenn Terry, who was hiding under a table with the legal .45-caliber semiautomatic pistol he'd been carrying.

It wasn't long before one of the robbers saw Terry under the table. As the man pulled his gun out, Terry shot him five times in the chest, killing him. The other robber, who'd been busy holding the restaurant manager hostage, fired at Terry, grazing him. Terry returned fire, killing him as well. Two bad guys dead, all of the good guys still alive.

In 2008, a man entered the Player's Bar & Grille in Winnemucca, Nevada. He shot two people from a family he was feuding with. Would he have shot others? We'll never know. A forty-eight-year-old man who was dining at the restaurant pulled out his handgun, which he was lawfully carrying with a Nevada license, and shot the attacker dead.

In 2012, just two days before the Sandy Hook murders, a potential mass murderer was stopped in an Oregon mall. The twenty-two-year-old man, who came armed with an AR-15, several loaded magazines, and a load-bearing vest, opened fire, killing two people with his first three shots. Witnesses say he fired at least sixty shots. The sheriff later said that the man's intention was to shoot "anyone in his line of sight. . . ."

While most people were running away, twenty-two-year-old Nick Meli, who was shopping with a friend and her baby, drew his licensed, concealed handgun. But Meli didn't fire right away, as he was concerned about missing the gunman and hitting an innocent bystander.

When the killer turned and saw Meli's gun aimed squarely at him he fired one more shot . . . right into his own head. There were estimated to be ten thousand people in the mall that day.

Did any of the people in these incidents absolutely, without a doubt, prevent additional deaths? It's impossible to know or to prove something that did not happen. The evidence says yes, and common sense tells us that there are probably many, many incidents that have been stopped that will never make it into any kind of national statistic. However, one thing is completely sure: contrary to what the controllists tell us, all of the people who had a gun in these incidents impacted their situation in a positive way. They didn't fire wildly into the air, or confuse the police, or have their gun taken from them and used by the killer—all things that we are told to expect when more people have guns.

REGARDLESS, IF WE REALLY WANT TO STOP GUN MASSACRES WE NEED TO BRING BACK THE ASSAULT WEAPONS BAN.

SENATOR DIANNE FEINSTEIN (D-CA):

December 17, 2012: "On the first day of the new Congress, I intend to introduce a [Federal Assault Weapons] bill stopping the sale, transfer, importation and manufacturing of assault weapons as well as large ammunition magazines, strips and drums that hold more than 10 rounds."

January 24, 2013: "I believe this bill is a big step toward ending the mass shootings that have devastated families across the country—from Newtown to Aurora, from Tucson to Virginia Tech, from Columbine to Oak Creek."

Dianne Feinstein might want to listen to Vice President Joe Biden, who, after meeting with Democratic senators about various gun control legislation, said, "Nothing we're going to do is going to fundamentally alter or eliminate the possibility of another mass shooting..."

Despite debating gun control for decades, Senator Feinstein (who was also the author of the 1994 Federal Assault Weapons Ban) refuses to accept reality: assault weapons bans do absolutely nothing, because "assault" weapons are not functionally different from any other semi-automatic weapons. More on that in a minute, but first let's look at the evidence.

Feinstein points to two studies by criminology professors Chris Koper and Jeffrey Roth for the National Institute of Justice to back up her contention that the previous ban reduced crime. On her website about the 2013 assault weapons ban she references a part of a 1997 study that, on its own, seems to be pretty conclusive: "Our best estimate of the impact of the ban on state level gun homicide rates is that it caused a reduction of 6.7% in gun murders in 1995 relative to a projection of recent trends."

It's unfortunate that Feinstein stopped reading after that sentence. After all, if she'd simply read the next two she might've come away with a very different impression:

> However, with only one year of post-ban data, we cannot rule out the possibility that this decrease reflects chance year-to-year variation rather than a true effect of the ban. Nor can we rule out effects of other features of the 1994 Crime Act or a host of state and local initiatives that took place simultaneously.

And this, one paragraph later:

> Using a variety of national and local data sources, *we found no statistical evidence* of post-ban decreases in either the number of victims per gun homicide incident, the number of gunshot wounds per victim, or the proportion of gunshot victims with multiple wounds. Nor did we find assault weapons to be overrepresented in a sample of mass murders involving guns. (emphasis added)

If this is the study that Feinstein is publicly citing, imagine what the studies she's ignoring must have found!

Koper and Roth smartly suggested in their report that it may take more time for a demonstrable impact to be seen. So, seven years later, in 2004, they studied the ban again and published a follow-up paper for the National Institute of Justice with fellow criminologist Dan Woods as a coauthor.

Nothing had changed. While reiterating that it may take more time to fully assess the ban, they nonetheless concluded: "[W]e cannot clearly credit the ban with any of the nation's recent drop in gun violence. And, indeed, there has been no discernible reduction in the lethality and injuriousness of gun violence. . . ."

And, perhaps the most damning quote of all: "Should it be renewed, the ban's effects on gun violence are likely to be small at best and perhaps too small for reliable measurement. AWs were rarely used in gun crimes even before the ban."

As talk about the 2013 ban began to heat up and the White House announced several proposals, the National Institute of Justice wrote a private memo titled "Summary of Select Firearm Violence Prevention Strategies"—eventually obtained by the media—that addressed each of the initiatives. To say they were unenthusiastic about the impact of the assault weapons ban would be an understatement:

> Prior to the 1994 ban, assault weapons were used in 2–8% of crimes. Therefore a complete elimination of assault weapons would not have a large impact on gun homicides. A National Academy study of firearms and violence concluded that the weaknesses of the ban and the scientific literature suggest that the assault weapon ban did not have an effect on firearm homicides.

Given how well that memo makes the case against the ban, I'm surprised Feinstein hasn't yet linked to it from her website.

▌ YOU ARE SO OUT OF TOUCH. EVEN THE MOST CONSERVATIVE MEMBER ▌
OF THE SUPREME COURT THINKS WE SHOULD BAN ASSAULT WEAPONS.

"Antonin Scalia, the most conservative member of the Court . . .
disagrees with [National Rifle Association executive vice
president Wayne] LaPierre on the Second Amendment. Scalia
does not believe that the right to bear arms is absolute."

—LAWRENCE O'DONNELL

"Your Second Amendment rights do not extend to allowing you the capacity
as a U.S. citizen to possess artillery capable of shooting an aircraft
out of the sky. And it's not very controversial that that's the case."

—RACHEL MADDOW

"Indeed, even conservative Justice Antonin Scalia conceded in his opinion
in *District of Columbia v. Heller* that 'dangerous and unusual weapons' of
the sort not 'in common use' by the public can be regulated or banned."

—THINKPROGRESS

*Even Scalia believes that "military-style" semi-automatic weapons
can be banned!*

That is pretty much what people like Lawrence O'Donnell and
Rachel Maddow are trying to say or imply when they offer up these
arguments. But while it's true that Justice Scalia's opinion in the
2008 *Heller* case states that some types of gun control are permissible, that hardly means, despite what O'Donnell and Maddow might
like, that he or the Court endorses bans on common firearms and
accessories, like AR-15 rifles and fifteen-round magazines.

But before we get to the validity of these quotes, let's take a
step back and review what Scalia and the Supreme Court actually
said about restrictions on the Second Amendment in their 2008
Heller opinion:

Although we do not undertake an exhaustive historical analysis today of the full scope of the Second Amendment, nothing in our opinion should be taken to cast doubt on long-standing prohibitions on the possession of firearms by felons and the mentally ill, or laws forbidding the carrying of firearms in sensitive places such as schools and government buildings, or laws imposing conditions and qualifications on the commercial sale of arms.

The Court also added a footnote: "We identify these presumptively lawful regulatory measures only as examples; our list does not purport to be exhaustive."

Each of the "presumptively lawful regulatory measures" mentioned in the decision tells us something about the meaning of the right to keep and bear arms.

First, there are "prohibitions on the possession of firearms by felons and the mentally ill." These are exceptions to the general rule that individual Americans have a right to possess arms. Of course, this exception makes sense only if there is a general rule that people can possess arms. If no individual has a right to own a gun, there would be no point in announcing a special exception for felons and the mentally ill.

The next exception they listed was that it's permissible to have "laws forbidding the carrying of firearms in sensitive places such as schools and government buildings." Again, the exception proves that there is a general rule under which individual Americans have the right to bear firearms in public places. The exception to that rule is "sensitive places." If Americans did not have the general right to carry firearms, there would be no sense in announcing a special exception about certain places where they *cannot* do so.

Last on the list of examples is "laws imposing conditions and qualifications on the commercial sale of arms." The Court did not elaborate, but the word *commercial* is important. It suggests that there might be constitutional problems with laws that impose "conditions and qualifications" on the *non*commercial transfer of firearms by private individuals. It's one thing for the government to regulate gun stores or home businesses that are routinely engaged in firearms commerce; it's another thing entirely to impose similar conditions and qualifications on private citizens who want to occasionally give or sell a personal firearm to a friend or family member.

But what about those outright bans? The part of *Heller* that seems to make controllists most euphoric is this quote: "[T]he Second Amendment does not protect those weapons not typically possessed by law-abiding citizens for lawful purposes, such as short-barreled shotguns." Using this reasoning, we might also say that poison gas and nuclear bombs are "not typically possessed by law-abiding citizens for lawful purposes," and so the possession of them is not protected by the Second Amendment.

But what about the other side of that quote? If the Constitution does not protect weapons that are *not* common, then doesn't it stand to reason that it *does* protect those weapons that are? After all, the *Heller* court struck down the D.C. handgun ban because it applied to "an entire class of 'arms' that is overwhelmingly chosen by American society for that lawful purpose" of self-defense.

Maddow is obviously right about people not being able to "possess artillery capable of shooting an aircraft out of the sky." But by using such an extreme example, she actually illustrates exactly why semi-automatics are permitted by the Constitution: artillery would clearly be considered, as the Court referenced, a "dangerous or unusual" weapon, one that, by any standard, is certainly not "in common use" by the public.

But that logic completely falls apart when you try to apply it to AR-15s or high-capacity magazines.

While the definition of an "assault weapon" is always changing based on the political winds, there are probably at least 10 million firearms that would be banned under Senator Feinstein's 2013 definition of "assault weapon." There are about 4 million AR-15 rifles in America.

Currently, about 82 percent of new handguns manufactured in the United States are semi-automatics. Many of them come with factory-standard (not "high-capacity") magazines of 11 to 20 rounds. For the AR-15, a 30-round magazine is standard. The number of magazines in the United States holding more than 10 rounds is likely in the tens of millions.

With that level of popularity and mass appeal, it'd be a big stretch to claim that any of these weapons and accessories is in any way "unusual" or not commonly used. So, with all apologies to MSNBC and the liberal blogosphere, Antonin Scalia is still not your friend.

▌NO CIVILIAN NEEDS A MILITARY-STYLE WEAPON. ▌

"Weapons of war have no place on our streets, or in our schools, or threatening our law enforcement officers."
—*PRESIDENT BARACK OBAMA*, February 4, 2013

"Weapons designed originally for the military to kill large numbers of people in close combat are replicated for civilian use."
—*SENATOR DIANNE FEINSTEIN (D-CA)*, January 24, 2013

"[The Newtown killer used] a weapon that was designed only to kill and maim people—not for hunting, not for recreation or competitive sport, but to kill and maim people at war. It's a military-style weapon."
—*SENATOR RICHARD BLUMENTHAL (D-CT)*, December 18, 2012

Have you ever stopped to think how powerful a particular word or phrase can be in shaping someone's response to an issue? Controllists have. That's why, when they talk about semi-automatic rifles, they intentionally use terms like "weapons of war" and "military-style."

A recent study done by psychologists at Stanford University measured the difference in response between the sentences: "Crime is a beast ravaging the city of Addison" and "Crime is a virus ravaging the city of Addison." After reading one of those sentences people were asked whether they'd support tougher law enforcement in an effort to control crime. The results reveal why controllists are so careful with their language: The group that read crime defined as a "beast" was 32 percent more likely to recommend tougher enforcement. The study authors wrote that "even the subtlest instantiation of a metaphor (via a single word) can have a powerful influence over how people attempt to solve social problems like crime and how they gather information to make 'well-informed' decisions."

This is why the term "gun control" is morphing into "gun safety." Jonathon Schuldt, a professor of communications at Cornell University, explained the rationale:

> In a nation where freedom is among the deepest ideals, control is almost a dirty word, and it is much easier to justify why one is against control than it is to justify why one is against safety.

A quick Google news search over headlines from the last few weeks reveals that this new terminology is spreading fast:

- CBS News: Biden on gun safety: No more excuses
- *Detroit Free Press:* Debate over gun safety, rights comes home to Oakland County

- *ThinkProgress:* Gun Safety Advocates Force NRA Backed Democrat out of Congressional Race
- *New York Times:* Biden Presses Senate Democrats to Support Gun Safety Agenda
- ABC News: Chicago officials push for new gun safety legislation

The same principle applies to this argument about "military-style weapons"—the term itself is an immediate tip-off as to the real motivation of these people. Keep an eye out for this kind of language when you hear gun control proposals from people who claim to be "reasonable"—it's an immediate tip-off as to their real motivation.

Putting aside the language games, the argument for banning the kinds of weapons that Obama, Feinstein, and Blumenthal are talking about is total nonsense. None of the weapons banned under the 1994 legislation or the updated version are, in fact, "military" weapons. In other words, they might *look* like menacing machine guns, but they fire only one bullet for each pull of the trigger.

The killer in Newtown used a .223-caliber Bushmaster rifle. This weapon bears a physical resemblance to the M-16, a machine gun that has been used by the U.S. military since the Vietnam War. It's frequently said that there is "no reason" for such "military-style weapons" as the Bushmaster to be available to civilians. But isn't that a lot like saying there is no reason why any civilian should drive a military-style car like the Hummer?

The key word, of course, is *style.* The Hummer may be military in style, but not in substance. Likewise, "assault weapons" like the Bushmaster may be similar to military guns in their cosmetics, but not in their operation. One pull of the trigger; one bullet.

In truth, an "assault weapon" is whatever the Dianne Feinsteins of the world say it is. They attempt to create federal bans that identify these weapons based on their cosmetic features, like barrel shrouds, folding stocks, pistol grips, etc., but none of these things have anything to do with the lethality of the weapon. It's almost like gun-discrimination: we treat weapons differently based solely on their outward appearance.

Fully automatic weapons (i.e., "machine guns") are, on the other hand, not military-"style" weapons; they are actual military weapons—and they've generally been outlawed for civilian use since 1986. While the media and controllists don't like to make that distinction clear, this debate has nothing to do with those weapons.

▐ YEAH, BUT IF YOU MODIFY ONE, IT BECOMES FULLY AUTOMATIC. ▐

> "The AR-15, when it's been modified by someone who knows what they're doing, can fire four to six bullets a second and 100 bullets in one minute. These are killing machines. They are machine guns."
>
> —*PIERS MORGAN, December 21, 2012*

In his zeal to illustrate how overly deadly the AR-15 supposedly is versus other guns, Piers has finally revealed that he has absolutely no idea what he is talking about.

Since an AR-15 fires rounds at the same rate as any other semi-automatic weapon (be it a handgun or one of those dreaded "assault rifles"), he has to resort to this idea of the gun's being "modified by someone who knows what they're doing." While he makes this sound easy, it's not—it effectively involves replacing the entire firing mechanism inside the gun.

But perhaps the best response to Morgan's argument is also the simplest one: twenty years in prison.

It is a federal felony to convert an AR-15, or any other gun, into a fully automatic weapon.

Period. End of story.

If we are really going to debate how criminals might access, modify, convert, or adapt guns to fit their needs, then we can put all of the other arguments behind us right now, because none of them make a difference.

That said, it's pretty telling just how weak your argument is when you have to resort to a "yeah, but criminals might ..." stance to make your point.

▌I STILL DON'T UNDERSTAND WHY ANYONE WOULD ▌NEED A SEMI-AUTOMATIC IN THEIR HOME.

"Why does anybody in America who is not in the military or the police force need a semi-automatic weapon that can unleash hundreds of shots in a matter of a few minutes and slaughter innocent Americans?"

—*PIERS MORGAN*, December 17, 2012

"Semi-automatics have only two purposes. One is so owners can take them to the shooting range once in a while, yell heehaw, and get all horny at the rapid fire and the burning vapor spurting from the end of the barrel. Their other use—their only other use—is to kill people."

—*STEPHEN KING*, Guns

I first want to offer my apologies to anyone who will read this section and say to themselves, *Yeah, no kidding, what idiot does not know that?* Unfortunately, there are plenty of people who either don't understand the way guns work, or who purposefully confuse their terminology to push an agenda.

The prefix *semi* comes from Latin and means "half." Replacing *semi* with *half* in some common English terms would give us *half-formal, half-final,* and *half-automatic.* A semi-formal dance does not require formal wear; a semi-final in basketball means you still have another game to play; and a semi-automatic guns means that your weapon cannot fire a hail of bullets for as long as you pull the trigger.

Semi-automatic guns are just as their name implies: semi-automatic. They can fire bullets as fast as one can pull the trigger. A semi-automatic does not fire anywhere near as quickly as a machine gun—otherwise known as a full-automatic weapon.

Those who have a primal hatred for semi-automatic rifles like the AR-15 usually aren't reasonable enough to have a real conversation with. Most of them simply want the gun banned, without any thought as to what the alternative might be. Unfortunately, unlike many other products, there is no "in-between" when it comes to guns. There is no type of gun that would fire faster than a manually loaded gun, but not as fast as a semi-automatic.

So, to answer the question posed by Piers Morgan and Stephen King as to why anyone would need a semi-automatic (and I hope you notice how both of them specifically use the term *semi-automatic,* which includes most modern handguns), it's because the alternative is either a revolver, which can be fired almost as fast and would therefore need to be banned as well, or a manual bolt-action gun that requires way too much time to reload. Even experienced shooters can easily take several seconds to pull the bolt back, load another bullet into the chamber, and close the bolt again. If you miss with your first shot (and probably give away your location in the process), or if you are facing multiple armed criminals, you may very well need to fire many rounds rapidly.

Some people consider that to be a dumb point. *What are the odds that you'll ever have to fend off multiple attackers or need to fire a bunch of shots?* Well, consider these seven cases, all from December 2012, the same month of the Newtown tragedy, where victims faced at least three attackers.

—Las Vegas, Nevada (December 24, 2012): "[F]our suspects—at least one of them carrying a firearm—knocked on the door of a first-floor apartment occupied by a couple and their infant. The assailants barged in when the woman occupant answered the door. The intruders were met with armed resistance." Police described the scene as involving "a multitude of gunfire." One of the attackers was killed and the three others fled and were at large.

—Sacramento, California (December 23, 2012): A home invasion robbery left one intruder dead and three other intruders injured. The home was serving as a day-care center and several children were inside when the attempted robbery occurred.

—Amarillo, Texas (December 19, 2012): A woman and her boyfriend arrived at her home to find several armed men inside. When the couple entered the home a gunfight ensued. One of the intruders was killed and the boyfriend suffered non-life-threatening injuries.

—Atlanta, Georgia (December 18, 2012): Very early on a Wednesday morning three men entered a home to commit a robbery. In the ensuing gunfight, one of the invaders was wounded and fled, though he was later arrested when he went to a hospital for treatment of his gunshot wound. Another robber jumped out a second-story window to escape, but he died from the fall.

—Boardman, Ohio (December 15, 2012): On a Saturday evening, four people tried to break into the home of James Truman. Two of the attackers had guns, and at least one of them fired shots. The homeowner was able to successfully drive the attackers away.

—Apple Valley, California (December 6, 2012): An "elderly man" is described as firing "multiple rounds" at three intruders who broke into his home. The homeowner found the criminals inside his home when he arrived at about 10 p.m. The newspaper report describes how the man's assailants tried to attack him from different sides, but that the homeowner was able to drive them out of the house.

—Oakland, California (December 3, 2012): Three armed men broke into a house on a Monday morning. The homeowner exchanged a large number of gunshots with the criminals, wounding one of them. Police later caught the other two.

This list is not meant to be comprehensive, but it should illustrate the idea that being attacked by multiple people—especially in cities where gangs are a problem—is not all that far-fetched. And to Stephen King, I hate to break it to you, but in the event people ever try to invade my home, you're right: my AR-15 semiautomatic has only one intended use: to kill them.

▌ I'VE HEARD THAT YOU PLAN ON DEFEATING THE ENTIRE ▌ UNITED STATES MILITARY WITH YOUR ASSAULT RIFLE.

"This is the survivalist argument that lies at the heart of the assault weapon defense: Being able to kill U.S. soldiers."
—*JOE SCARBOROUGH*, January 15, 2013 (via Twitter)

"If you're girding yourself for a massive battle with a despotic black copter über-government, stocking up on guns, ammo, and Campbell's' Cream of Mushroom soup, and it doesn't happen, then you just look like an a**hole with a soup fetish. . . . The only way that your life would end up being truly meaningful is if the tyranny talk comes true, which puts you in the difficult position of having to argue tyranny hypotheticals."
—*JON STEWART*, January 17, 2013

"[I]n their view, to do right by the Constitution you and I need to be able to defeat the U.S. military in battle. We need to be able to overthrow the U.S. government. . . . This is not hyperbole if you believe the gun radicals' philosophy about guns—that gun rights are to protect our ability to overthrow the government—then we need to be able to destroy the U.S. military so we can overthrow that government. . . . [I]s that what gun rights are for?"
—*RACHEL MADDOW*, January 14, 2011

It's amazing what a few hundred years can do to perspective. When the Founders added the first ten amendments to the Constitution in December 1791, they included the right to bear arms because it was *necessary to the security of a free state.* Put yourself in their shoes: after establishing the first-ever society meant to be governed *by the people*, not by some monarch or despot, they were understandably more than a little paranoid about a tyrannical government performing an *Extreme Makeover: Dictator Edition.*

Two hundred and twenty-one years (and no monarchs, kings, or dictators) later, the idea that Americans would ever need to bear arms against a tyrannical government is used quite literally as a punch line. Those who talk about it are usually mocked, belittled, and ridiculed by the controllists. And since government tyranny is now a thing of the past, they argue, what other possible reason could there be to own a "killing machine" like an AR-15?

Well, Joe, Jon, Rachel—I'm glad you brought it up. This "gun radical" is more than happy to explain it to you. As comical as the idea may seem to you guys as you sit in your Manhattan office towers, the primary objective of gun rights is to protect American citizens against a tyrannical government. You can laugh all you want—but the unarmed and vulnerable masses in the former Soviet Union, fascist Italy, and Nazi Germany weren't laughing as they and their friends and families were sent to their mass graves. (Yes, I did get the memo that talking about genocides allegedly makes you sound even crazier—but I shredded it.)

The people who mock this idea usually rely on a few standard tricks to make the whole concept seem ludicrous. One of those tricks is to paint a battle scene in which a lone person is trying to fight against the *entire government.*

You want an assault rifle so that YOU can take on the entire United States military? That is ridiculous!

I completely agree, that is ridiculous. I would definitely not be able to defeat the United States military in battle. In fact, if disaster strikes and Rachel, Jon, and Joe evacuate Manhattan and come take refuge on my ranch, I probably won't even be able to protect them from roving bands of gangs looking for food. But the best part about the Second Amendment is that, as long as it exists, I will probably never have to try. Any government would be certifiably insane to attempt to overrun a country composed of 80 million people owning 300 million firearms.

If a government is someday dumb enough to attempt it, at least citizens stand a fighting chance. To head off the usual retort, yes, the U.S. military does have tanks and jets and bombs—so what? The odds that an armed citizenry is ever taking on the armed forces as we know them today are Powerball-winning small. If things were ever to get to the point where armed conflict became necessary—especially if the underlying issue was an abandonment of the Constitution by our leaders—we'd likely see most soldiers refuse to fight or even flip sides and join the masses.

Of course, those are hypotheticals that do nothing to make the case anyway. People who believe that to be a laughable scenario (and I agree that, right now, it is) will never be convinced, because they don't want to be. For the rest of us, the Second Amendment is the ultimate deterrent, a German shepherd sitting on the front porch, frothing at the mouth and barking like mad.

If we continue to stand for our rights, none of us alive today will ever have to pick up a weapon against our government. The bad news is that if those rights are watered down or taken away, the risk of tyranny will increase with each passing generation.

In the meantime, there are plenty of other reasons why a law-abiding American household may choose to have a semi-automatic gun like an AR-15 in their home. During the 1992 Los Angeles race riots, hundreds of violent looters targeted average citizens and businesses. According to the History Channel:

> Traffic was blocked, and rioters beat dozens of motorists, including Reginald Denny, a white truck driver who was dragged out of his truck and nearly beaten to death by three African-

American men. . . . Los Angeles police were slow to respond, and the violence radiated to areas throughout the city. California Governor Pete Wilson deployed the National Guard at the request of Mayor Tom Bradley, and a curfew was declared. By the morning, hundreds of fires were burning across the city, more than a dozen people had been killed, and hundreds were injured.

Rioting and violence continued during the next 24 hours, and Korean shop owners in African-American neighborhoods defended their businesses with rifles. On May 1, President George [H. W.] Bush ordered military troops and riot-trained federal officers to Los Angeles and by the end of the next day the city was under control. The three days of disorder killed 55 people, injured almost 2,000, led to 7,000 arrests, and caused nearly $1 billion in property damage, including the burnings of nearly 4,000 buildings.

Sounds like fun. How would you like to have been a business owner in that area armed with nothing more than a baseball bat or a single-shot pistol? Think you'd stand much of a chance against a violent mob? And what about those who were trapped in the aftermath of Hurricane Katrina, when armed looters ruled streets that had been virtually abandoned by police?

"It's downtown Baghdad," tourist Denise Bollinger said about New Orleans. "It's insane."

"The looting is out of control. The French Quarter has been attacked," Councilwoman Jackie Clarkson said. "We're using exhausted, scarce police to control looting when they should be used for search and rescue while we still have people on rooftops."

If you're caught in the middle of that, what do you do—just dead-bolt your door and hope for the best? Maybe pull out that antique six-shooter against a violent gang of looters?

In the New York City area, Hurricane Sandy proved to many who had previously scoffed at the so-called survivalists just how fast civilization and the rule of law can break down. After just a few days of no electricity, gas lines began to stretch for miles. In New Jersey, state troopers were deployed to all stations along the major interstates to calm nerves. In New York City a man had a gun stuck in his face at a Queens gas station after complaining that another customer had cut him off in line. A Lowe's store manager in New York said, "You see the worst in people at a time like this. We're trying to be there for them, but they get angry when they can't get batteries or flashlights."

That was less than a week without electricity—what happens in a real, long-term disaster? What happens when food supply lines get cut off, or an epic storm cuts a large swath of people off from the outside world? Would you rather be hunkered down with a handgun holding a maximum of seven rounds (which is now the limit in New York), or an AR-15 with a magazine large enough to ensure that your entire family is protected?

I could go on—but here's the thing: I don't have to. As of now this is still a free country and I have a right to defend myself and my family as I see fit. I do not need to come up with a list of justifications to make New York media elitists like Piers Morgan, Rachel Maddow, and Jon Stewart happy.

All I need is the Second Amendment—just the way it is.

▌ I'M GLAD YOU BROUGHT THE SECOND AMENDMENT UP ▌ AGAIN. YOU HAVE TO ADMIT THAT IT'S PRETTY OUTDATED.

"I don't think the Founding Fathers had the idea that every man, woman, and child could carry an assault weapon."

—*MAYOR MICHAEL BLOOMBERG*, December 16, 2012

"When they passed the 2nd Amendment, they had muskets. It took 20 minutes to load one, and half the time, you missed, OK? The 2nd Amendment didn't take into account assault weapons. . . ."

—*DEEPAK CHOPRA*, December 21, 2012

> "[T]hey always hide behind the Second Amendment. They're fabulous at
> doing that. But the Second Amendment does not give you the right to bear
> any kind of arm. And technology has changed. And, of course, the design
> has changed. The proficiency of the manufacturing has changed."
>
> —*ED SCHULTZ*, December 19, 2012

This is a pretty popular argument that's made all the time by those who really want to click their heels together three times and pretend that the Founders were imbeciles who had no clue that technology would ever advance. Fortunately, it's also an argument that's been roundly rejected by a little group called the United States Supreme Court.

In the landmark 2008 ruling *District of Columbia v. Heller,* the Court observed:

> Some have made the argument, bordering on the frivolous, that only those arms in existence in the 18th century are protected by the Second Amendment. We do not interpret constitutional rights that way. Just as the First Amendment protects modern forms of communications, e.g., Reno v. American Civil Liberties Union, 521 U. S. 844, 849 (1997), and the Fourth Amendment applies to modern forms of search, e.g., Kyllo v. United States, 533 U. S. 27, 35–36 (2001), *the Second Amendment extends, prima facie, to all instruments that constitute bearable arms, even those that were not in existence at the time of the founding.* (emphasis added)

That is such a clear and resounding quote that it's probably counterproductive to even attempt to add to it, but there are a few other things that the mayor, Deepak, and Ed would be wise to understand.

It is true that the people who wrote and ratified the Second

Amendment did not specifically intend to protect the AR-15 or other modern-day weapons. It's also true that there was no specific intent in the First Amendment to protect the right to say whatever you want on the Internet or to broadcast ridiculous opinions on MSNBC. And when our Founders wrote the Fourth Amendment they had no idea that they'd someday be protecting the right to talk privately on a cell phone (although whether or not the government is actually respecting that right is for another book).

Anyone who claims that weapons like semi-automatics are so modern and unique that the Second Amendment does not apply to them would also have to believe that the First Amendment protects only writing done with quill pens on parchment paper, since those were the norm back then. How could we expect the Founders to have ever imagined the world we live in today?

We couldn't—but there is a good reason why the Second Amendment was not written to say "the right of the people to keep and bear muskets, flintlock pistols, and swords"—the types of weapons that were common in 1791. The Founders, far from being the idiots the media paints them to be, knew that technology would evolve. That's why they wrote the amendment to protect "arms" as a class and it's why the Constitution as a whole defines a relationship between individuals and the government that is applied across time—no matter what technology eventually brings us.

Let's go back to the First Amendment to illustrate what might happen if we were to take the Bloomberg/Chopra/Schultz view. At the time this amendment was written, a skilled printer could produce 250 sheets in two hours. Today, a modern newspaper printing press can produce 70,000 copies of an entire newspaper in an hour. And, with digital publishing, a newspaper article can be read globally within minutes after it is written.

One consequence of this technological evolution is that an irresponsible media can cause far more harm today than it could in 1791. For example, in 2005, *Newsweek* published a story claiming that American personnel at Guantánamo Bay had desecrated Korans belonging to prisoners there. The magazine eventually retracted the story, but it had already spread worldwide, setting off riots in six countries and resulting in the deaths of at least seventeen people.

Had *Newsweek* been using eighteenth-century printing presses, the false story would have been read by several thousand people confined to a small geographic area. It would have been months—if ever—before the *Newsweek* issue with the false story was read by anyone in Pakistan or Afghanistan.

This is the same basis upon which the Bloomberg/Chopra/Schultzes of the world argue that we should ban innovations in the firearm industry, like semi-automatic rifles and large-capacity magazines. *Look at the damage they can inflict!* these people argue. But that point of view is held only by people who have no respect for the Second Amendment and its key role in preserving freedom. After all, if you believe in the Second Amendment as strongly as you believe in the First, then these kind of innovations aren't dangerous—they're necessary. A mass printing press or a racist Internet blog in the hands of a madman can inflict serious harm on society; but banning either of those things inflicts much more.

Those who believe that freedom of the press is a basic tenet of a free society look at things differently. Instead of opposing any change that makes the press more "lethal," they embrace it. *More speech, not less.* That is common sense to most progressives—yet they can't seem to bring themselves to apply that same standard to the very next amendment.

Aside from theoretical debates about the application of freedoms across time, the assumption about what our Founders knew about guns at that time is totally wrong. While weapons that could fire multiple shots without reloading were crude, they were not unheard-of and it would not take someone of the intelligence of James Madison to realize that they were the future. As professors Clayton Cramer and Joseph Olson pointed out in their paper "Pistols, Crime, and Public Safety in Early America," "Repeating, magazine-fed firearms date back to at least the 1600s; concealable 'pepperbox' handguns firing five to seven shots without reloading were in use by the end of the eighteenth century."

There was still plenty of room for improvement in multi-shot guns, and those improvements were eagerly anticipated. As Cramer and Olson wrote, "In 1791, it is clear that the goal of multi-shot firearms was on the mind of gunsmiths, inventors, and shooters. . . . Guns were in hand and getting better with every generation. Inventors knew where they wanted to be. . . ."

It was only a few years after the Bill of Rights was ratified that a big change came to American firearms. In 1798, Eli Whitney became the first American industrialist to secure a government contract for mass production of firearms (ten thousand units) using interchangeable parts. Suddenly, gun making was no longer a one-at-a-time business of craft production.

By the early nineteenth century, interchangeable parts were used routinely and Whitney's "American system of Manufacture" was soon being copied around the globe. The United States, whose main exports up to that point had been crops and other raw materials, entered the industrial revolution with guns blazing—literally. Firearms quickly became America's first mass-production export.

The nineteenth century saw enormous improvements in firearms technology—much faster loading, more reliable ignition, more and better multi-shot firearms. Before the twentieth century dawned, semi-automatics were well developed and ammunition had taken the modern form that we still see today.

As far as we can tell from the historical record, nobody ever asserted that these improvements in firearms technology somehow meant that the Second Amendment would no longer apply. And that's because nobody was dumb enough to believe that to be true.

▮ EVEN IF THAT'S TRUE, EVERYONE AGREED THAT THE ▮ SECOND AMENDMENT WAS ONLY ABOUT MILITIAS.

"For a hundred years, the Constitution was interpreted to mean that state militias, essentially state police, had a right to bear arms, because that's what the first half of [the] Second Amendment says. But, as of 2008, as a result of years of lobbying and years of Republican appointees to the court, in 2008, the Supreme Court said individuals have a right to bear arms under the Second Amendment."

—*JEFFREY TOOBIN*, December 18, 2012

If constitutional law were a game of poker, Jeffrey Toobin would be a world champion. He is able to easily bluff when his hand is terrible, and he can do it with complete seriousness and conviction. He's also sly. If the game isn't going in his direction, he'll look for some loophole he can use to change the rules.

I have nothing against Toobin personally, but I do have something against revisionist history. You'll notice, for example, that Toobin specifically used the phrase "For a hundred years" at the start of that quote, meaning that he's talking about the time from 1908 through 2007. But the Second Amendment was adopted in 1791. What happened to those 117 years from 1791 through 1907? Should we just pretend they don't exist? Toobin doesn't say.

No wonder. From the ratification of the Second Amendment through the end of the nineteenth century, nearly everyone— American courts, legal scholars, and the public—understood that the Second Amendment protects an individual right to keep and bear arms. The concept of a "a well-regulated Militia" was very important, but it was understood that a militia could exist only if the people from whom it would be drawn possessed their own arms and had plenty of opportunity to use and practice with them.

But let's put all of that aside for a moment and play by Toobin's rules. We'll assume that the first 117 years after 1791 don't count and we'll look *only* at the century before the landmark 2008 *Heller* decision.

Toobin believes that the Second Amendment protects a right belonging to state governments rather than to individual citizens. This theory was popular for part of the twentieth century, especially among uninformed talking heads and those with such a white-hot hatred for gun ownership that they could not fathom the Framers' wanting individuals to own arms. It was not, however, very popular with the Supreme Court.

Let's start by taking a closer look at *Heller*. The five-justice majority (led by Justice Scalia) followed what is called the "standard model" of the Second Amendment—essentially that it protects the right of law-abiding persons to have firearms for legitimate purposes, especially for self-defense.

The four dissenting justices (led by Justice John Paul Stevens) instead utilized what is called the "narrow individual right" theory, which says that the Second Amendment protects an individual right, but only in connection with service in a well-regulated militia. The *Heller* dissenters did not clarify the extent of that right, except to say that they believe it does not include owning a handgun for personal self-defense.

Justice Stephen Breyer wrote a dissent that was joined by the three other dissenting justices: "[B]ased on our precedent and today's opinions, to which I believe the entire Court subscribes: (1) The Amendment protects an 'individual' right—i.e., one that is separately possessed, and may be separately enforced, by each person on whom it is conferred."

In other words, all nine justices, including those who were not, as Toobin put it, "Republican appointees," agreed that the Second Amendment protects some sort of individual right. Yet, according to Toobin, this was apparently the first time in the last century that anyone had interpreted it that way. That just doesn't add up. So let's take a look at the history and try to find the truth.

First, a decision in Toobin's favor—though it was just outside of his hundred-year window. In *Salina v. Blaksley* in 1905, the Kansas Supreme Court ruled that the right to arms in the Kansas Bill of Rights meant only that the state militia, in its official capacity and while in actual service, could not be disarmed. The court also said that the Second Amendment meant the same thing. The problem is that no other court adhered to the *Salina* approach until 1935, when federal district judge Halsted Ritter (who was later removed from office) wrote that the Second Amendment "refers to the militia, a protective force of government; to the collective body and not individual rights."

The U.S. Supreme Court's one major Second Amendment case of the twentieth century was *United States v. Miller* in 1939. The Court essentially ruled that only weapons useful to the militia are protected by the Second Amendment, but the Court did *not* say that individuals have a constitutional right to possess those protected weapons *only* while serving in the militia.

Confused yet? It gets worse before it gets better.

After *Miller,* some lower courts did come close to adopting Toobin's "states' right" theory. In 1942, for example, the federal Third Circuit Court of Appeals decided that the Second Amendment "was not adopted with individual rights in mind, but as a protection for the States in the maintenance of their militia organizations against possible encroachments by the federal power."

This seems to imply that the right to arms is truly collective, since this decision implied that states could essentially supersede federal law by creating their own militia-based firearm laws. That would mean that Texas could declare all able-bodied men to be part of their militia and arm them with machine guns so that they would be ready to fight the feds. The Third Circuit apparently did not recognize the implication of its theory, and neither does Toobin.

The federal Gun Control Act of 1968 greatly expanded federal gun laws. As a result, defendants (usually convicted felons) who had been arrested for gun possession began to be marched in front of federal courts. Since the guilt of these defendants was not usually in question, attorneys sometimes resorted to the argument that the gun ban itself violated the felons' Second Amendment rights. The lower courts rejected these arguments, sometimes declaring that the Second Amendment protects a state's right, and sometimes that it protects a "collective" right.

The New Jersey Supreme Court was the first to use the actual term *collective right*, when, in 1968, it upheld the state's new gun licensing statute in *Burton v. Sills*. The New Jersey court maintained that the Second Amendment "was not framed with individual rights in mind. Thus it refers to the collective right 'of the people' to keep and bear arms in connection with 'a well-regulated militia.'"

With the legal history of the Founding era and the nineteenth century having been forgotten, the opinions of judges like Halsted Ritter were presented as mainstream consensus, rather than as the outliers they really were. Although regular Americans continued to believe that the Constitution guaranteed their individual right to own firearms, controllists were sensing blood in the water and began to push the collective theory hard. Inside the self-important, elitist Manhattan cocktail party circuit, the term *col-*

lective right was the new go-to attack on anyone who dared raise a hand in support of their natural and constitutional rights.

But not in the Supreme Court. In the 1990 case *United States v. Verdugo-Urquidez* (which actually involved a Fourth Amendment question) Chief Justice William Rehnquist's majority opinion clarified that "the people" whose right to arms is protected by the Second Amendment are "persons." Not—as Toobin claims—state governments who want to have state militias.

Other Supreme Court opinions in the time between *Miller* (1939) and *Heller* (2008) also recognized an individual right. For example, in *Poe v. Ullman* (1961), Justice John Harlan's celebrated dissenting opinion analyzed the individual "liberty" that the Fourteenth Amendment protects from state government infringement. Among the many parts of that "liberty" were "the freedom of speech, press, and religion; the right to keep and bear arms; the freedom from unreasonable searches and seizures; and so on."

Justice Harlan's language about the Second Amendment was later quoted with approval in several subsequent Supreme Court cases, including Justice Sandra Day O'Connor's opinion for the Court in *Planned Parenthood v. Casey* (1992); in both the majority and the dissent in *Moore v. East Cleveland* (1977); and in Justice Potter Stewart's concurrence in *Roe v. Wade* (1973).

In other words, Toobin has history wrong. There were plenty of opinions over the last century—from very reputable people—that the Second Amendment protects an individual right. By the time *Heller* rolled around, the "collective right" theory was so outdated that only one of the sixty-seven amicus briefs filed in the case (a brief that counted Janet Reno and Eric Holder among its authors) referenced the concept. The justices themselves dismissed the idea out of hand—leaving Toobin alone to revise history so that it fits his own conceptions.

▌ MOST GUNS KEPT IN THE HOME ARE USED FOR ▌ SOMETHING OTHER THAN SELF-DEFENSE.

"But there is a more fundamental problem with the idea that guns actually
protect the hearth and home. Guns rarely get used that way. In the 1990s, a team
headed by Arthur Kellermann of Emory University looked at all injuries involving
guns kept in the home in Memphis, Seattle and Galveston, Tex. They found
that these weapons were fired far more often in accidents, criminal assaults,
homicides or suicide attempts than in self-defense. For every instance in which a
gun in the home was shot in self-defense, there were seven criminal assaults or
homicides, four accidental shootings, and 11 attempted or successful suicides."

—NEW YORK TIMES, editorial, February 2, 2013

Totally false.

Unfortunately, this Kellermann study (which, by the way, is twenty years old) has received widespread attention and has probably scared lots of people away from keeping a gun in the home for self-defense.

As with any study that is often cited by people trying to score political points, it's helpful to take a step back and ask some commonsense questions about the approach. Here is how it worked: After someone was killed in or near their home, Kellermann and his coauthors would go ask their relatives if a gun had been kept in the home. If the relative said yes, researchers then simply *assumed*—yes, *assumed*—that it must have been the very same gun that was used in the killing.

In very few cases was the researcher able to actually trace the homicide to the gun kept in the house. Out of the 444 cases they analyzed, there were only eight instances in which "the investigating officer specifically noted that the gun involved had been kept in the home." (If anything, this research ought to be interpreted as showing that guns kept at home are seldom used against the owners.)

The Kellermann study—which did not look at any other defensive gun uses (for example, incidents where a gun was effective after merely being brandished) except those where someone was shot—also compared the data on homicide victims with a so-called control group of similar individuals living within a mile of the victim. Researchers offered these folks ten dollars and then asked them whether they had guns and whether they had suffered any homicides. Unsurprisingly, researchers found that there were fewer homicides and fewer guns in the control group than in the other group. There was, in other words, a correlation between gun ownership and homicide.

Kellermann and his coauthors took this to imply that gun ownership *causes* more homicide. But, remember, the first group had specifically been chosen because a homicide had occurred. *These were not randomly selected households.* It is very likely that this group of homicide victims faced an increased risk of death compared to other similar people—which may very well be why they chose to have a gun at home in the first place.

Using this same logic, one could easily interview people who've been shot while wearing a bulletproof vest and conclude that these vests are very dangerous. Or you could interview people who died after calling 911 and conclude that calling the police often leads to death. These comparisons are idiotic—you are selecting a group of people who are already at risk.

Kellermann and his coauthors are medical doctors. So, for the fun of it, let's use their incredibly irresponsible method to "prove" that hospitals are dangerous places.

To start, we'll collect data just as these researchers did. We'll get a list of all the people who died in a particular county over the period of one year, and then we'll ask their relatives about whether those people had been admitted to a hospital during the previous year. Next, we'll find people of similar demographic (age, sex, race, neighborhood, etc.) characteristics who are still alive and we'll ask them whether they'd been to a hospital over the last year.

What do you think we might find? In all likelihood we would expose a very strong correlation between the amount of time one spends in a hospital and the probability of subsequently dying. But would that be evidence that hospitals kill people or would it be evidence that you are a really stupid researcher?

It obviously makes no sense to compare the life expectancy of a sick person who felt the need to go to the hospital with that of a healthy person. To get a fair result you would need to compare two *equally sick* people where one goes to the hospital and the other does not. Likewise, to get a fair result in the gun study, a researcher would need to select two similar groups beforehand, give guns to one group but not the other, and then track each of these groups over a significant period of time. That, of course, is how medical trials are done.

Putting aside the Kellermann "study," there are other important considerations to make on this topic, such as government-imposed restrictions on the storage and use of guns in the home.

Two economists, John Lott and John Whitley, have studied in depth the effects of government-imposed restrictions on the use of guns. They found that new policies meant to lower gun ownership rates, or new "safe storage" rules that forced people to lock up their guns, were followed by criminals becoming more likely to attack people in their homes and that those attacks were more likely to be successful. The abstract of their study, published in 2001 by the *Journal of Law & Economics,* sums up their findings well:

> It is frequently assumed that safe-storage gun laws reduce accidental gun deaths and total suicides, while the possible impact on crime rates is ignored. We find no support that safe-storage laws reduce either juvenile accidental gun deaths or

suicides. Instead, *these storage requirements appear to impair people's ability to use guns defensively.* Because accidental shooters also tend to be the ones most likely to violate the new law, *safe-storage laws increase violent and property crimes against law-abiding citizens* with no observable offsetting benefit in terms of reduced accidents or suicides. (emphasis added)

With fewer guns in people's homes, murders, rapes, robberies, and aggravated assaults all rose. And when trigger lock laws prevented guns from being readily accessible for immediate self-defense, crime rates rose, too. Lott's study projected that, five years after all states implemented new "safe storage" laws, there would be 355 more murders and almost 5,000 more rapes in the United States.

▌ KEEPING A GUN AT HOME IS POINTLESS ANYWAY. ▌

"Most home invasion victims with arms find themselves in Herbert Clutter's position: surprised and overwhelmed. Unless you sleep with your .45 auto fully loaded and under your pillow, you're apt to find yourself in the same position if the bad guys ever should show up in your bedroom, enquiring as to the location of your safe."

—*STEPHEN KING*, Guns

King is referencing a 1959 attack on the Clutter family (also the subject of Truman Capote's book *In Cold Blood*), where two men invaded a home in Holcomb, Kansas, and killed the entire family. His point, I guess, is that since Herbert Clutter had guns in his house but was unable to use them before being killed, no one should have guns in their house. He also offers up absolutely no evidence to back his assertion that "most" home invasions end that way.

Let's pretend for a second that Stephen King is completely right and that "most" home invasion victims never have a chance to get to their gun before they're killed. Does that really mean that no one should have a gun in their house? What about the people who aren't in that "most" category—does King prefer that they'd ended up like the Clutters?

Besides, King is using just one example of a crime where having a gun might make a difference. There are plenty of others. Some say that none of these situations can be made better by a victim having a firearm, but the data says that's just not true. And, data aside, there's a larger reason why owning a gun for self-defense makes sense: it's our responsibility to protect our families and neighbors.

Milwaukee County sheriff David Clarke Jr. created quite a stir recently when he voiced a commercial making it clear that we all have a role to play when it comes to defending ourselves against criminals:

> I am Sheriff David Clarke, and I want to talk to you about something personal, your safety. It is no longer a spectator sport. I need you in the game. But are you ready? With officers laid off and furloughed, simply calling 911 and waiting is no longer your best option. You can beg for mercy from a violent criminal, hide under the bed, or you can fight back. But are you prepared? Consider taking a certified safety course in handling a firearm so you can defend yourself until we get there. You have a duty to protect yourself and your family. We are partners now. Can I count on you?

The sheriff is making an important point. Police are vital in helping to protect people's safety, but they can't be there all the time. In fact, even in times before budget cuts and furloughs and the like, police generally don't arrive until after a crime has already been committed. When you have to face a criminal by yourself, the sheriff is absolutely right: you have a duty to protect yourself and your family. The best way to do that is with a firearm that you've been trained how to use.

Controllists often debate with hypotheticals about what might go wrong if someone keeps a gun in their house, but the data is actually pretty clear. The Department of Justice has been surveying 100,000 to 150,000 people a year for the National Crime Victimization Survey (NCVS) for thirty years, with about 4,000 to 6,000 being victims of violent crimes. This survey includes extremely detailed data on these victims, from the type of crime, to where and when it occurred, to the characteristics of the criminal and victim, to how the criminal responded when attacked.

When you analyze this data, the results are extraordinarily clear: the best way to ensure your own safety when attacked is to have a gun, and know how to use it. The injury rate for victims of assault who use a gun is about *half* the rate for victims who try to run away, and about one-tenth the rate for those who did not try to protect themselves in any way.

A 2000 study published in the *Journal of Criminal Justice* looked at NCVS data over a nine-year period to determine what the consequences of armed victims really were. The study's summary makes their findings clear:

> [Crime victims] who had and used guns had both lower losses and injury rates from violent crimes. . . . Based on these findings, consequences of having a greater portion of potential victims being armed were analyzed. Results showed this would reduce both losses and injuries from crime, as well as a criminal's incentive to commit violent crimes and to be armed.

▌ OKAY, BUT THAT DOESN'T APPLY TO WOMEN. THEY'RE STILL ▌ MORE LIKELY TO BE KILLED WHEN THERE'S A GUN IN THE HOME.

"There's good evidence that a gun in the home increases the likelihood that a woman in the home will die. There is no evidence that a gun in the home is protective for the woman."

—DAVID HEMENWAY (director of the Harvard Injury Control Research Center), January 31, 2013

Seriously? There's no evidence that guns help protect women? Maybe Hemenway needs to leave that Harvard campus on occasion and get out into the real world (where about 15 percent of our military is female) to see what is happening. Here are just a few of the many cases involving women and guns from one recent month:

—Magnolia, Texas (January 29, 2013): Three male burglary suspects forced themselves into a home with a mother and her six-year-old child inside. The mother fired her pistol, hitting one of the invaders, at which time all three criminals then fled the scene.

—Milwaukee, Wisconsin (January 9, 2013): When a robber pulled a knife and threatened a female clerk, she pulled a gun and the attacker ran away.

—Loganville, Georgia (January 4, 2013): A woman hiding in her attic with her two children shot an intruder multiple times before fleeing to safety. The woman had tried to hide from the man, but he searched the house until he found her. She fired six shots, hitting him five times. She ran out of bullets but bluffed that she would continue shooting if he came any closer, at which point he fled the home.

And it's not just older women who use guns defensively. Here's a case from last fall involving a young girl.

—Durant, Oklahoma (October 19, 2012): A strange man rang the doorbell of a twelve-year-old girl's house. When she didn't answer he went to the back door and kicked it down. The girl called her mother, who told her to get the family's gun, hide in the closet, and call 911. When the man tried to enter the closet she was hiding in she shot and wounded the man.

I understand that, compelling as it is, this is all just anecdotal evidence, so let's turn back to the Justice Department's National Crime Victimization Survey to see what the data says about attacks specifically on women.

It's not even close. The probability of serious injury from aggravated assault is 2.5 times greater for women who offer no resistance than for women who resist their attacker with a gun. In contrast, the probability of a woman's being seriously injured was almost four times greater when resisting without a gun than when resisting with a gun.

While both men and women benefit from having a gun, the benefit for women is much larger. The reason for that is pretty simple: Attackers are almost always men, and the difference in strength between a male attacker and a female victim is bigger, on average, than the difference in strength between a male attacker and a male victim. Having a gun therefore makes a bigger relative difference for a woman than it does for a man.

You can also see this difference with people who carry concealed handguns. According to research by John Lott, murder rates decline when either sex carries a concealed gun, but the effect is particularly pronounced for women. An additional woman carrying a concealed handgun reduces the murder rate for women by three to four times more than an additional armed man reduces the murder rate for men.

So women and guns are not oil and water, far from it—but let's address Hemenway's quote specifically because he seems to be alluding to domestic violence incidents that occur in the home. In that case, women shouldn't be fearful of a gun in the home; they should be fearful of dating or marrying men with criminal records.

Murders of wives by their husbands by any means are, thankfully, relatively rare. While the FBI doesn't break down its data by the type of weapon used, about 4.6 percent of all murders (603) in 2010 involved wives being murdered by their husbands. Given the number of married women (about 63,150,000 million), the overall rate was infinitesimally small (0.0009 percent).

But this is not really the right statistic to be looking at. The focus should not be on the gun, but the man. Few murderers are committed by previously law-abiding citizens. While studies are hard to come by, a 1988 report looked at the largest seventy-five counties in the United States and found that approximately 90 percent of adult murderers had previous criminal records as adults. A 1983 study by Gary Kleck and others looked at national data. They wrote: "The FBI is rather vague about the types of crimes for which offenders were previously arrested or convicted. However, in special computer runs for the 1968 Eisenhower Commission it was determined that 74.7 percent of persons arrested between 1964 and 1967 for criminal homicide had a record of previous arrests for 'a major violent crime or burglary.' " But they made another important point as well: "Because most violent acts are not reported to the police, and many do not result in any kind of officially recorded action (arrest, conviction, or imprisonment), official records of the previous violence of homicide offenders represent only the tip of the iceberg."

The bottom line is that a criminal record is usually more of a risk factor for violence than is gun ownership—especially when those guns are owned legally.

▌ FORTY PERCENT OF ALL GUNS ARE SOLD ▌ WITHOUT BACKGROUND CHECKS.

"But it's hard to enforce that law when as many as 40 percent of all gun purchases are conducted without a background check. That's not safe. That's not smart. It's not fair to responsible gun buyers or sellers. . . ."

—*PRESIDENT BARACK OBAMA, January 16, 2013*

"40 percent of all gun trades, there's no background check."
—*PIERS MORGAN*, December 21, 2012

**"40 percent of gun sales now take place privately, including
most guns that are later used in crimes."**
—NEW YORK TIMES *(editorial)*, January 14, 2013

I could probably fill the rest of this book with quotes from gun control activists using some version of this same statement. It's been printed in the *New York Times, USA Today,* and the *Wall Street Journal*. Even on the normally skeptical Fox News channel, we heard Chris Wallace asserting that "in 40 percent of the [gun] sales there is no such screen on the person buying the gun." Senator Chuck Schumer (D-NY) went even further, claiming that the number is actually "48 percent of gun sales."

It is repeated so often that it's now mostly accepted as fact even though most people who use it have no idea where it originally came from. Even more troubling is that this shocking "fact" provided the principal rationale for the president's first announced gun control proposal: "universal background checks." After all, if current gun purchase rules are so lax that almost half of all weapons are obtained without a background check, then there would seem to be much room for improvement.

The truth, however, is that this statistic is way off. The real number is likely less than 10 percent. I'll explain in a bit, but first some background on where the "40 percent" number comes from.

In 1997, the National Institute of Justice (NIJ) undertook a study on gun ownership using data collected from a telephone survey done in 1994. (There's the first red flag: these numbers are nearly twenty years old.) The survey, which included 2,568 households, asked several questions about gun ownership—including how the guns were obtained.

Of those people who told the researcher how they obtained their gun (second red flag: only 251 of the 2,568 people answered this question), 35.7 percent said they acquired it from someone other than a licensed dealer. This number has conveniently been rounded up to 40 percent as the years have passed. According to a PolitiFact analysis of the underlying data in this survey, researchers in some cases "made a judgment call" when respondents weren't clear about where they obtained the gun.

So, we already have four big problems with this number (it's a twenty-year-old number based on answers from just 251 people that was rounded up to 40 percent for no good reason and was subject to the "judgment" of researchers), but there are many more.

Problem five is that this statistic pertains to *all transfers* of firearms, not just purchases, which is the term the president used. A very large portion of guns change hands through inheritances and gifts. Grandpa's old rifle ends up with a grandchild; a husband gives his wife his old handgun for protection, etc. In the 1994 survey, 29 percent of people who answered the question about the origin of their gun said it came from a family member or friend.

Common sense tells us that the government is not going to be able to impose background checks on those transfers (and, if fact, even President Obama's background check proposal excludes gun transfers within a family). If a husband has purchased a gun from a licensed dealer and has cleared the background checks, the gun will physically be at the home anyway and nothing would prevent his spouse from using it as well. Who technically "owns" the gun is a moot question.

The *Washington Post*, at the prompting of John Lott, asked the researchers who originally wrote the 1997 NIJ study to rerun their numbers, looking only at the origin of gun purchases instead of all transfers. When they did, things changed quite a bit. The *Post* summarized the new results:

> [R]ather than being 30 to 40 percent (the original estimate of the range) or "up to 40 percent" (Obama's words), gun purchases without background checks amounted to 14 to 22 percent. And since the survey sample is so small, that means the results have a survey caveat: plus or minus six percentage points.

So now, with the margin of error, we are down to as low as 8 percent, and we haven't even gotten to the biggest problems yet. For example, the vast majority of the purchases disclosed in the original survey (at least 80 percent) were reportedly made *before* the Brady Act instituted mandatory federal background checks on February 28, 1994. Prior to this act, federal law merely required people to sign a statement that they had not been convicted of certain crimes or had a history of significant mental illness. Many people who filled out these forms likely did not consider them to be the equivalent of a "background check." Given the system put in place after Brady, we should expect a much higher percentage of gun owners to now say that their purchase was subject to a background check than they did back then.

The seventh problem with the survey is that it asked buyers if they *thought* they were buying from a licensed firearms dealer. Back then there were more than 283,000 federally licensed gun dealers (FLLs), while today there are just 118,000. Many people who bought from these "kitchen table" FLLs did not realize that they were buying from a fully licensed dealer because the transaction seemed so casual. The perception was that only "brick and mortar" stores were fully licensed.

No one knows exactly how many gun transactions are outside the FFL system today, but—excluding family gifts and inheritances—it's hard to believe that it is anywhere near 40 percent. And if someone does decide to study the issue again, I sincerely hope that this time they'll talk to more than 250 people.

While the 40 percent statistic clearly does not add up, what *really* doesn't add up is the language used by those who like to cite it. For example:

—**Mayor Michael Bloomberg:** "The loophole is called the gun show loophole."

—**Mayor Cory Booker (Newark, New Jersey):** "We've got to end the gun show loophole."

—**Ed Schultz:** "Closing the gun show loophole would be a big step forward because that's 40 percent of the sales in this country."

The "gun show loophole"? It doesn't exist. The laws at a gun show are the same as the laws everywhere else: licensed dealers must run background checks; private sellers (those not engaged in the business of selling firearms) do not. Any sale, by anyone, in any place is still subject to federal law requiring that guns cannot be sold to known criminals.

Calling private, noncommercial sales a "gun show loophole" is only meant to rile people up who have never been to a gun show. Controllists hope people hear about a loophole and picture criminals fresh out of prison loading up their trunks with AR-15s.

▌ **GUN SHOWS ARE WHERE CRIMINALS GET ALL THEIR WEAPONS.** ▌

"The overwhelming majority of my gun crimes and the overwhelming majority of gun crimes committed in America are done by people who get guns illegally, by people who get guns in the secondary market. That's what I said before. About 40 percent of our guns are being sold in secondary markets, places like gun shows, the Internet, there's no regulation, there's no background checks."

—*MAYOR CORY BOOKER, December 17, 2012*

It's just not true. In fact, even if you look at the flawed 1994 survey, only 4 percent of people said they got their firearm at a gun show. And another NIJ study, while admittedly pretty old (it's from the mid-1980s), found that, as Independence Institute gun policy scholar David Kopel put it, "gun shows were such a minor source of criminal gun acquisition that they were not even worth reporting as a separate figure."

Gun shows have never been a significant source of guns for criminals. Under President Clinton the Bureau of Justice Statistics conducted a survey of eighteen thousand state prison inmates in 1997. Fewer than 1 percent of inmates (0.7 percent) who said they had a gun reported that they'd obtained it from a gun show.

As I said before, when gun control groups refer to "gun shows" what they really are talking about is the private transfer of guns. Eighteen states regulate the private transfer of handguns— some of those regulations go back more than several decades. Not surprisingly, just as with semi-automatic weapon bans, there is not a single, credible academic study showing that these regulations reduce any type of violent crime.

The survey also exposed another ugly by-product of Clinton-era gun control regulations: those who were big gun dealers back then became registered firearms dealers, but the push to make licensing harder left many private individuals who'd previously sold a gun here or there without one.

▌ EVEN A MAJORITY OF NATIONAL RIFLE ASSOCIATION ▌ MEMBERS SUPPORT UNIVERSAL BACKGROUND CHECKS.

"[W]hen Republican pollster Frank Luntz asked NRA members earlier this year whether they support background checks on every gun sale, 74 percent agreed."

—*ARKADI GERNEY*, former manager of Mayors Against Illegal Guns,
December 16, 2012

"Overwhelmingly, 84 percent of gun owners in America—82 percent of gun owners in America, 74 percent of NRA members believe that should change. Changing that alone, ending those secondary markets, makes a difference."

—*MAYOR CORY BOOKER*, December 19, 2012

With all the misinformation out there about background checks, from the shocking claim that "40 percent of all gun purchases are conducted without a background check" to Senator Chuck Schumer's erroneous claim that background checks have "blocked 1.7 million prohibited individuals from buying a gun" (these were just initial denials, not people prohibited from ever buying a gun), it isn't surprising that many polls have found strong support for "universal background checks." But it's the claim that "NRA members" overwhelmingly support universal background checks that has proven to be sensational enough to make headlines and be used by controllists. Like all widely quoted statistics that sound counterintuitive, this one is worth taking a closer look at.

The poll in question was done in May 2012 and was commissioned by Mayors Against Illegal Guns—a group overwhelmingly made up of anti-gun Democrats and founded by gun-hating Mayors Bloomberg of New York City and Thomas Menino of Boston in 2006.

The survey itself was conducted by Frank Luntz, a pollster and Republican consultant who runs those focus groups during elections on Fox News. According to the PBS show *Frontline*, Luntz's real specialty, however, is "testing language and finding words that will help his clients sell their product or turn public opinion on an issue."

I'm not big on attacking the messenger when you don't like the message, but given Luntz's supposed "specialty" it's worth noting that his studies have been questioned before. In 1997 he was reprimanded by the American Association for Public Opinion

Research (AAPOR) because he "repeatedly refused to make public essential facts about his research."

The association explained: "AAPOR tried on several occasions to get Luntz to provide some basic information about his survey, for example, the wording of the questions he used. For about a year, he ignored these requests."

To summarize, the guy whose specialty is words refuses to disclose his.

Why am I bringing this up? Because the exact same issue seems to have resurfaced again. According to the *Washington Post,* which reported on the survey, Luntz's group "did not provide requested details about the poll's question wording."

That's a pretty big issue, considering the type of question we are talking about here. If you want us to believe that NRA members overwhelmingly support universal background checks, you'd damn well better be willing to tell us how you asked the question. To ask people if they support "background checks on the sale of guns" is not quite the same thing as asking if they support background checks on private transfers within a family or between neighbors or friends.

Aside from the question itself, there are a couple of other red flags. For example, the *Washington Post* reported that the survey "used a non-random opt-in Internet panel to contact self-identified NRA members." Self-identified? It gets worse: "The Luntz poll of 945 gun owners nationwide . . . was divided evenly by gun owners who were current or lapsed members of the NRA and non-NRA gun owners."

Okay, so now it's "self-identified" current or lapsed NRA members—you can see why people might have questions about the accuracy of the results.

Even if you believe in Luntz and his surveys it's still clear that Bloomberg's group has done some cherry-picking. In an earlier 2009 survey conducted by Luntz for the same group, only 26 percent of non-NRA members and 16 percent of NRA members agreed that they "feel that the laws covering the sale of guns should be more strict." And a recent poll of *current* members done for the NRA by AG Research found that just 5 percent support "[a] new federal law banning the sale of firearms between private citizens." That's relevant considering that there would be no way to enforce universal background checks if someone could legally sell a gun to their friend, outside of the system.

The point is that the wording of the question is pertinent to understanding what people really believe about this issue. Since the results of polls that *have* disclosed their wording differ so markedly from the Luntz poll that controllists love to cite, we can only assume that the Luntz poll used some creative wording to get their desired results.

THE NRA IS THE POSTER CHILD FOR BAD RESEARCH.

ALAN DERSHOWITZ:

"[John Lott's research] is junk science at its worst. Paid for and financed by the National Rifle Association. . . . [The NRA] only funds research that will lead to these conclusions."

—July 23, 2012

"[W]hat's happening is the NRA is buying their data. They're buying their facts. They're hiring and commissioning so-called scholars to come up with the kinds of lies."

—December 18, 2012

The only specific name that Professor Dershowitz ever seems to offer as an example of his allegations is John Lott. Dershowitz seems to have a problem with the conclusion reached by Lott's study of right-to-carry (RTC) laws in the 1990s, when Lott was a scholar at the University of Chicago Law School—though Dershowitz won't say exactly what that problem is, other than to call the findings "junk science."

Others disagree with Dershowitz. For example, the late James Q. Wilson, who was often described as the preeminent criminologist in the United States, dissented from a report on firearms and violence published by the National Academy of Sciences in 2004. Wilson found that, while there might be disagreement over some types of crime, "the evidence presented by Lott and his supporters suggests that RTC laws do in fact help drive down the murder rate."

If you want to dismiss Wilson's dissension and instead rely on the committee report, you find that they are basically asking for more data. They say that the current results are "highly fragile" because some studies reach differing conclusions and some do not include enough years. While that's not a ringing endorsement, it's a long way from there to the "junk science" charge leveled by Dershowitz.

But, really, none of this should be very surprising. The idea that more guns could mean less crime is counterintuitive to everything that controllists believe. It doesn't matter what the data says, or how many times it's reviewed and verified, because they will *always* find a way to dismiss it.

Attacks on Lott, especially over his alleged "NRA funding," regularly pop up in the gun control debate and are regularly debunked. (Dershowitz has, of course, never provided any evidence of his claims.) A recap of the debunked charges is included in the sources at the end of this book, but the bottom line is that Lott was a scholar at the University of Chicago Law School, which does not take gun lobby contributions. Each of the three editions of the book he wrote based on his research (*More Guns, Less Crime*) has been peer-reviewed by multiple academics from across a range of specialties and published by the University of Chicago Press.

The most ironic part of this is that, in contrast to funding by gun control advocates like the Joyce Foundation (where Obama used to serve on the board of directors), there is actually a *lack* of specific funding for gun research coming from any "conservative" groups. If there is bias in what gun research has revealed, Dershowitz would be better served to look at the left-wing wealthy donors who are funding so many of the lies and discredited research that make their way into the mainstream media.

▌THE 2004 REPORT SAID WE NEED MORE DATA AND RESEARCH▌ ON GUNS—AND THEY'RE RIGHT, WE NEED TO KNOW MORE.

"We need objective scientists looking at all the variables, not looking at kind of pat points being sponsored by the NRA or supporters of the NRA, not pseudo-scientists who come to the problem with the point of view. We need the National Science Foundation, we need other objective scientists looking at everything, looking at the relationship between the amount of guns in society and the amount of crime holding constant racial factors, financial factors, economic, all kinds of other factors. We need to learn the truth about this. We have to follow the facts and follow the truth. And the truth doesn't come from the NRA, the truth doesn't come from alleged professors who have a point of view and who have been advocating a particular point of view about this. It comes from objective scientists. We need to know the truth, lives depend on it."

—*ALAN DERSHOWITZ*

There's a big difference between not *knowing* the truth and not liking it. In this case, Dershowitz falls into the latter category—which is not be surprising, considering that he believes gun control is the "single most effective way to reduce crime" and has said that "the pervasiveness of guns in our society is destroying America."

He's clearly not an independent analyst on this, but that doesn't necessarily make him wrong. The facts are what make him wrong.

Virtually everything that Dershowitz says we need to research has already been researched. Scientists and scholars have looked at all of the relationships he mentions, using extensive law enforcement variables (arrest, execution, imprisonment rates, different types of policing strategies, unionization of police forces, and even hiring and promotion rules for police), income and poverty measures (poverty and unemployment rates, per capita real income, as well as income maintenance, retirement, and unemployment payments), the thirty-six measures of demographic changes (by age, gender, and race), along with the national average changes in crime rates from year to year and average differences across states. In addition, estimates made in prior research account for the differences in various concealed-handgun laws and twelve other types of gun control laws (background checks, gun show regulations, assault weapon bans, penalties for using guns in a commission of a crime, waiting periods, stand-your-ground laws, gun lock laws, and so on).

Is it really possible that Dershowitz hasn't read any of the research that he is commenting on? Is it really possible that he doesn't know that the National Research Council, which conducts many studies "mandated and funded by Congress and federal agencies," produced a comprehensive report on gun violence in 2005? Is it really possible that his statements are true—that *no* "objective scientists" have *ever* researched gun violence in a serious way? Or, is it more likely that he just doesn't like how all of that research turned out?

■ **MORE GUNS MEANS MORE CRIME. ANY DATA TO THE** ■
CONTRARY IS A LIE OR NRA PROPAGANDA.

"We don't need people carrying guns in public places. That's not what
the founding fathers had in mind. It doesn't add to anybody's safety.
Quite the contrary, it makes us have a much more dangerous society."
—*MAYOR MICHAEL BLOOMBERG*, December 16, 2012

"One thing I would suggest is it's time for us—everybody hates commissions,
but it's time for us to have a commission of 10 great distinguished scientists
to put the lie to this notion of more guns, less crime. I know the statistics.
I know the FBI data. I teach it. But most Americans believe the NRA
propaganda. The NRA buys scholars. They buy statistics. It's just wrong."
—*ALAN DERSHOWITZ*, January 7, 2013

Professor Dershowitz might be an extremely well-known, well-spoken, and brilliant professor, but he is a *lawyer,* not a statistician. He seems to have very little clue as to what he is talking about when it comes to the gun debate and the effects different laws have had in different places.

Despite his convincing rhetoric, the truth is that Dershowitz has never written a statistical paper. A careful listener should notice that he merely makes grandiose assertions and avoids referencing the precise studies or numbers that would back them up. If he knows the FBI data so well, then why doesn't he tell us the actual numbers instead of just saying that everything else is wrong?

We'll get back to that data in a second, but first I have to hand it to Dershowitz for his suggestion that we should create a commission to settle this. I mean, what could go possibly go wrong with that? We just find ten totally independent, well-respected scientists who have absolutely no preconceived notions about guns or political agendas. That should be easy.

This commission idea is a pretty well-known method of quelling debate. *Look at what the commission said; case closed!* I have no doubt that many control advocates would love nothing more than to get their hands on a final commission report recommending draconian restrictions or outright gun bans. In fact, the only way these people can win this argument is by claiming that the science is settled.

Dershowitz also conveniently seems to forget that, as I mentioned earlier, a National Academy of Sciences commission already has taken a hard look at the data. During the final days of the Clinton administration this panel reviewed 253 journal articles, 99 books, and 43 government publications, along with some of its own empirical work on firearms and violence. Their 2004 report was not able to identify a single gun control regulation (for example, background checks, gun buybacks, assault weapon bans, limits on gun sales, regulating gun dealers) that clearly reduced violent crime, suicide, or accidents.

Considering the work this panel has already done, it's obvious that Dershowitz doesn't want a commission; he wants a commission that will reach a different conclusion.

But let's put all of that aside and instead look at the crux of his argument, which is that all the data is wrong and all the studies are biased.

First, since he specifically said he "knows" and "teaches" the FBI data, we'll start there. The FBI's *Uniform Crime Reports* detail the number of "Firearms-Related Murder Victims" per capita. If the "notion that more guns, less crime" is the lie that Dershowitz claims it is, then we should very clearly see this firearm murder rate moving higher through the years as more and more firearms make their way out into the public.

But exactly the opposite happens.

Below is a table that lists the best government estimates of the number of firearms in America along with the per capita firearm murder statistics from the FBI.

Firearm Murders Per Capita vs. Total Civilian Firearms in America			
Year	Per-Capita Firearm Murder Victims	Total Firearms in the U.S.	Source of Firearm Estimate
1993	6.6		
1994	6.3	192 million	Nat'l Inst. of Justice
1995	5.6		
1996	5.0	242 million	ATF
1997	4.6		
1998	4.1		
1999	3.7		
2000	3.6	259 million	ATF
2001	3.6		
2002	3.8		
2003	3.8		
2004	3.6		
2005	3.8		
2006	3.9		
2007	3.9	294 million	ATF
2008	3.6		
2009	3.4	310 million	ATF
2010	3.2		
2011	3.2		

Notice anything strange about those numbers? The firearm murder rate keeps falling even as the number of total firearms in America keeps rising.

I understand enough about statistics to know that a table

like this is prone to all sorts of problems. The Dershowitzes of the world would say that you can't just look at overall trends like this because you have to control for all those variables he alluded to in his other quote. Fine, and that's been done plenty of times in other peer-reviewed studies—but this data, covering eighteen years of history and using only the most respected federal sources, sure puts, to use a term that Dershowitz knows well, the burden of proof squarely back on those who make the claim that the correlation between these numbers is actually the *complete opposite* of what the FBI data shows.

This correlation can also be found in states, like Virginia, where the total number of firearms per 100,000 residents was up 63 percent over five years, but where total gun-related violent crimes fell 27 percent over that same period. Virginia Commonwealth University professor Thomas Baker, who ran the study, told the Richmond Times-Dispatch that the data, "seems to point away from the premise that more guns leads to more crime, at least in Virginia. . . . From my personal point of view, I would say the data is pretty overwhelming."

Right-to-Carry Laws

One way that researchers determine the effectiveness of gun control is by looking at right-to-carry (also sometimes known as "concealed carry") laws. These are basically laws that allow, with some exceptions, people to keep a weapon on them in public areas. There are several varieties of these laws, including "unrestricted" (no permitting required), "shall-issue" (you need a permit but it's pretty much a formality—governing bodies are not allowed to use their own discretion), and "may-issue" (a permit is necessary and may be granted only if you meet certain requirements or conditions).

A lot of sophisticated studies have been done on this topic and they virtually all reached the same conclusion: violent crime falls after right-to-carry laws are adopted, with bigger drops the longer the right-to-carry laws are in effect.

While there is tons of evidence to support this conclusion, some of the most interesting is produced when you compare changes in crime rates in adjacent counties on opposite sides of state borders. In general, the county in the state that adopts a right-to-carry law sees a drop in violent crime, while the adjacent county in the state without the right-to-carry law sees a slight increase.

The evidence that right-to-carry laws work is so persuasive that someone attempting to identify some other factor that's responsible for the results would have to answer these questions:

—Why does the impact of this new factor increase over time?
—Why is this new factor so well correlated with the rate at which right-to-carry permits are issued in different states?
—Why would this new factor have a greater impact on violent crime relative to property crime and on individual murders relative to mass (multiple-victim) public homicides?
—Why does this new factor affect adjacent counties on opposite sides of state borders differently?

Various academic scholars have studied the impact of letting citizens carry concealed handguns on crime rates. Eighteen recent studies have found that right-to-carry laws deter violent crime. Ten studies have claimed either small benefits or no effect.

Dershowitz, however, is not convinced. He apparently believes that the findings below, from those eighteen different studies (in addition to the opinion from James Q. Wilson that was previously quoted) performed by different scholars at different times, were all bought and paid for by the gun lobby.

- John Lott and John Whitley find that "the longer a right-to-carry law is in effect, the greater the drop in crime."

- The third edition of John Lott's *More Guns, Less Crime* found that the states which issued the most permits had the biggest drops in violent crime rates. Lott also found: "By any measure, concealed-handgun permit holders are extremely law abiding."

- Economists Florenz Plassmann and Nicolaus Tideman found that "right-to-carry laws do help on average to reduce the number of these crimes."

- Carl Moody, chair of the economics department at the College of William and Mary at the time of the study, said his findings "confirm and reinforce the basic findings of the original Lott and [David] Mustard study."

- In another paper that studies county crime rates from 1977 until 2000, coauthored by Moody and attorney and sociologist Thomas Marvell, the authors write that "the evidence, such as it is, seems to support the hypothesis that the shall-issue law is generally beneficial with respect to its overall long run effect on crime."

- Economists Eric Helland and Alex Tabarrok studied county crime rates from 1977 to 2000 and concluded that "shall-issue laws cause a large and significant drop in the murder trend rate" and that "there is considerable support for the hypothesis that shall-issue laws cause criminals to substitute away from crimes against persons and towards crimes against property."

- David Olson, a professor of criminal justice at Loyola University Chicago, and Michael Maltz, a professor of criminal justice at the University of Illinois at Chicago, found "a decrease in total homicides" driven by a drop in gun killings.

- Bruce Benson, a Florida State economics professor, and social scientist Brent Mast found that their results "are virtually identical to those in [Lott and Mustard's study]."

These researchers have used a variety of approaches: different statistical techniques, different data sets, different control variables, or a variety of specifications. Yet, despite all these alternative set-ups, the general conclusion is the same: right-to-carry laws reduce violent crime.

Some studies have reached the opposite conclusion. A 2011 paper published in *American Law and Economics Review* claimed, "the most consistent, albeit not uniform, finding to emerge from both the state and county panel data models conducted over the entire 1977–2006 period with and without state trends and using three different specifications is that aggravated assault rises when RTC laws are adopted. For every other crime category, there is little or no indication of any consistent RTC impact on crime."

Sounds impressive, except that a review of this study by four researchers, including John Lott, found the results to be based on a data set that included significant errors (for example, it accidentally counted the same county seventy-three times), as well as a significant arrest-rate error that severely biased the results toward finding a negative effect from right-to-carry laws. A later addendum to this paper admitted the errors and claimed that the underlying results were still valid. But researchers like John Lott, who routinely confirm the findings of other studies in this field, disagree, and have not been provided access to the data used to reach these conclusions.

▌ THE REASON NOTHING CHANGES IS THAT ▌
THE NRA BUYS OFF POLITICIANS.

"I have been stunned by the sheer political cowardice of so many politicians in America who seem just terrified of saying anything that the NRA may object to. The NRA has four million members. America has 310 million people living here. I just don't understand why everybody is so coward[ly] about publicly debating this and trying to get exactly the measures in place that you've [Connecticut Senator Richard Blumenthal] just suggested."

—*PIERS MORGAN*, December 20, 2012

"Let's talk political reality. I don't have to tell you, the NRA has a lot of clout on Capitol Hill. In the last election cycle, they contributed $20 million to campaigns last year. Fifty percent of the members of the new Congress have an A-rating from the NRA."

—*CHRIS WALLACE*, February 3, 2013

It is often hard for gun control advocates to accept that everyone wants the same thing: to save lives and reduce violence. President Obama believes that those "pundits and politicians and special interest lobbyists" who oppose his gun control regulations do so "because they want to gin up fear or higher ratings or revenue for themselves." That they will do "everything they can to block any commonsense reform" that is necessary "to protect our communities and our kids."

I take that not only as a personal insult, but as akin to the president essentially saying that I put ratings and profit above the lives of children. Nothing could be further from the truth, and it's those kinds of reckless statements that make both sides dig in their heels. After all, I may believe that Obama's views on guns are dangerous and that his policies endanger public safety, but that's quite a bit different from accusing him of personally benefiting from the deaths of innocent children.

Obama's mind-set explains why so many of those "pundits and politicians" on his side of the aisle refuse to accept that there are voters and politicians who oppose more gun control laws. It isn't because the NRA has bought them off; they don't buy votes, they invest in politicians who already believe that the right to bear arms is essential to our freedom.

Ironically, one of the best arguments *against* the Piers Morgans and Barack Obamas of the world on this topic comes from Alan Dershowitz, a guy who probably agrees with almost all of their gun control ideas. In response to Morgan's saying that the issue is that the NRA wields too much power, Dershowitz disagreed:

> I don't think it's the NRA power. I think it's people like us, not the two of us, but Americans who care about guns aren't doing enough to make our case to the public.
>
> Because we think it's their issue. We've given that issue over to them because they have lobbyists they pay money. But in the end, the people determine the outcome. . . . [W]e have a right to define the America we want to live in and we have the obligation to win politically, to vote for people to put gun control as a high priority.
>
> They [people who support the Second Amendment] put it as a number one priority. We who favor gun control put it as a 16th or 17th priority. So it's our fault, not the NRA's fault.

I knew that Dershowitz and I would find some common ground. He's right that, as with every controversial issue, it's ultimately up to the people and the voters to prioritize how much they care about it. Believe me, if this country was really anti-gun, you'd see things change very fast. But that's just not the case.

There is plenty of polling on this, but for a good example, take a look at the trend in those answering "yes, there should be" to this question that Gallup has been asking Americans since 1959: *Do you think there should be a law banning the possession of handguns, except by the police and other authorized persons?*

—1959: 60 percent
—1965: 49 percent
—1975: 41 percent
—1988: 37 percent
—1999: 34 percent

—2006: 32 percent
—2009: 28 percent
—2012: 24 percent

What about making it "illegal to manufacture, sell, or possess semi-automatic guns known as assault rifles?" (This question began in 1996).

—1996: 57 percent were for this idea.
—2004: 50 percent
—2012: 44 percent

The problem isn't the NRA; it's that the controllists refuse to admit that they themselves are out of step with the American people. And while Piers Morgan points out that the NRA has "only" 4 million members—as if that somehow implies they should not wield the power they do (for context, the ACLU claims about 500,000 members)—that in no way means that NRA members are the only Americans who want to protect their Second Amendment rights. A recent poll revealed that 68 percent of all Americans—not just gun owners—believe that "the constitutional right to own and carry a gun is as important as other constitutional rights, such as freedom of speech and freedom of the press." The Bloombergs of the world who live in their ivory castle and travel with armed security simply cannot understand why any of those simple-minded folk out in the heartland might ever want a gun themselves.

Finally, Chris Wallace's comment about the NRA contributing "$20 million to campaigns last year (2012)" just doesn't hold up. According to the Center for Responsive Politics, the NRA made just over $1 million in donations to specific candidates during the 2012 election cycle. The top recipients got $9,900.

Perhaps, to give Wallace the benefit of the doubt, he didn't really mean the money the NRA gave "to campaigns" but the total money they spent on all independent efforts. In that case his number is much closer—but it's not really fair to claim the NRA is buying politicians when the vast majority of that money never goes to the campaigns. Will the NRA support your reelection if they believe you support them? Of course—but isn't that the way it should be? The AFL-CIO spent nearly $9 million last election cycle, all in support of Democrats who support them, or against Republicans who don't. No one seems to have an issue with that.

▌ THE NRA IS SO CRAZY THAT THEY ACTUALLY WANT TO ARM OUR KIDS! ▌

ALAN DERSHOWITZ: "And when the NRA gets up and says the solution to it is to arm teachers in elementary schools and give kids guns—"

MORGAN: "—wild west. It's lunacy."

DERSHOWITZ: "We don't want to live there."

You're right, Alan, we don't want to live there. Fortunately, we don't have to because this is a lie.

Dershowitz is a great lawyer—he knows how to mix in just enough truth with his lies to get the jury to bite. But I'm not biting. For anyone interested in the truth, here is what Wayne LaPierre, executive vice president of the NRA, actually said:

Now, the National Rifle Association knows there are millions of qualified active and retired police, active reserve and retired military, security professionals, certified firefighters, security professionals, rescue personnel, an extraordinary corps of patriotic, trained, qualified citizens to join with local school officials and police in devising a protection plan for every single school.

We could deploy them to protect our kids now. We can immediately make America's schools safer relying on the brave men and women in America's police forces. The budgets—and you all know this—everyone in the country knows this—of our local police departments are strained, and their resources are severely limited, but their dedication and courage is second to none and they can be deployed right now.

I'm not seeing the part where LaPierre says that we should hand out guns with lunch, but maybe I just missed it. Oh, and Alan, in case you were wondering, putting armed, trained personnel in schools is not exactly a new concept. According to Mo Canady, executive director of the National Association of School Resource Officers, this idea was first proposed in the 1950s and was federally funded by the Clinton administration.

▌ COLUMBINE PROVES THAT PUTTING ARMED ▌ GUARDS IN SCHOOLS JUST DOESN'T WORK.

"Armed guards in schools? Hmmmm . . . Oh! That's why the 2 armed guards that were at Columbine HS that day were able to prevent the 15 deaths?"

—*MICHAEL MOORE*, December 21, 2012

"[Columbine] had armed guards and it didn't stop the tragedy."

—*DENNIS VAN ROEKEL* (president, National Education Association), December 27, 2012

I hear this argument all the time and there are several problems with it. First, the obvious one: you don't take one data point and dismiss an entire idea because of it—especially if you are serious about keeping kids safe. If you're going to tell me that the Columbine attack succeeded despite armed guards, you better tell me about the instances that failed because of them. Remember Vice Principal Joel Myrick in Mississippi? He stopped a killer by running to his car to grab a gun. What if it had been in his office instead? What if Pearl High School had been staffed with an armed cop? We'll never know—but don't bring up Columbine unless you're willing to talk about all of them.

But my main problem with this argument is that it's really just not true. At least not in the way they try to make it seem. Here's a condensed version of what really happened that day according to the Jefferson County, Colorado, Sheriff's Office:

Sheriff's Deputy Neil Gardner, a fifteen-year veteran of the Sheriff's Office, was assigned as a "community resource officer" to Columbine High School. He normally ate lunch in the cafeteria with the kids, but on that day, he ate in his car alongside the campus supervisor. The two men were monitoring students in an area called the "smokers' pit."

Around 11:23 a.m., a custodian radioed to Gardner, "Neil, I need you in the back lot!" Gardner started his car and pulled out onto the road. Another call, this one over his police radio, followed: "Female down in the south lot of Columbine High School." Gardner, believing that a girl had been hit by a car, put on his lights and siren and began to make his way toward that parking lot.

As Gardner pulled into the lot he saw kids running, smoke pouring from the school, and he heard several explosions and gunfire. Another message then came over the school radio: "Neil, there's a shooter in the school."

Gardner began to get out of his car but was immediately bombarded with gunfire. According to the report: "Eric Harris turned his attention from shooting into the west doors of the high school to the student parking lot and to the deputy." After firing approximately ten shots his gun jammed and Gardner returned fire. Harris eventually reloaded and began firing again before eventually retreating back into the school. (This exchange may have proved valuable, as it delayed the killers on their way to the school library, where the bulk of the killing occurred.) Very soon after that, additional backup began to arrive on the scene.

Two things stand out from this report: First, there were not "2 armed guards" at the school that day; there was one. And second, while Michael Moore is technically correct that the guard was "at" Columbine High School, he was not "in" it. To use this as the prime example of why armed guards in schools won't work is pretty disingenuous.

Unfortunately, many controllists suffer from magical thinking. They believe that banning guns will somehow make them safer, as though laws are all we need to stop criminals. But consider for a second that you felt threatened for some reason and then ask yourself this: would you feel safer with a sign on your front window saying "This house is a gun-free zone" or with an armed guard on call whenever you were home?

If you wouldn't put this sign on your home, why would anyone think it's okay to put them in places where young children gather nearly every day?

❙ COLLEGE STUDENTS ARE TOO IRRESPONSIBLE TO CARRY GUNS. ❙

"Carrying guns on a college campus, for example, is one of the dumbest things I've ever heard of in my life. I don't remember what you were like when you were in college, but I shouldn't have had a gun when I was in college nor should anybody I knew. We just don't need guns every place."
—*MAYOR MICHAEL BLOOMBERG, December 16, 2012*

Currently, once someone qualifies for a permit in a right-to-carry state they can carry a concealed handgun with them virtually anywhere in that state except for a few designated gun-free zones. Prominent among those "protected" areas are universities and schools.

As of the beginning of 2013, five states guaranteed people the right to carry concealed handguns on university campuses: Colorado, Mississippi, Oregon, Utah, and Wisconsin. Twelve other states, including two large ones, Texas and Florida, are currently engaged in a debate over whether to end their bans on concealed-carry on campus. Twenty-one states leave the decision up to individual schools, though it's not surprising that most liberal universities have views similar to Mayor Bloomberg's.

So, what about those views? Is Bloomberg right? Would armed students and faculty pose a danger to others? Would armed students confuse police and possibly get shot themselves?

Fortunately, we don't have to guess at the answers since many campuses have allowed concealed-carry for years, especially prior to the major push for gun-free zones back in the early 1990s. According to John Lott, "Back then, in the states that allowed concealed permitted handguns, students and professors frequently carried handguns, and there simply weren't any problems."

As a group, permit holders (not just those on college campuses) are exceedingly law-abiding. Consider the two states at the front of the current debate over carrying guns on campus: Florida and Texas, both of which keep detailed records on the behavior of their permit holders. Over the nearly twenty-five-year period from October 1, 1987, to June 30, 2012, Florida issued permits to 2.4 million people, with the average person maintaining that permit for more than a decade. Few of them—168 to be exact (about 0.01 percent)—have had their permits revoked for any type of firearms-related violation. (Ironically, the most common reason for revocation was carrying a concealed handgun into a gun-free zone, such as a school or an airport.)

Over a forty-three-month period—the latest period that data was available for—only four Florida permit holders had their permit revoked for a firearms-related violation—an annual rate of

0.0001 percent. The numbers are similarly small in Texas. In 2011, there were 519,000 active license holders. One hundred twenty of them were convicted of either a misdemeanor or a felony in that year, a rate of 0.023 percent—and only a few of those crimes involved a gun.

While it's clear that permit holders have succeeded in stopping a wide range of public massacres, at schools and elsewhere, there has not been a single reported incident where a permit holder has accidentally shot a bystander. Likewise, the police have *somehow* managed to get to the attackers without shooting any permit holders in the process.

Data and studies aside, there are also plenty of examples from the real world. Recently, Joe Salazar, a Colorado state representative, invoked the wrath of lots of people with this idiotic comment about why women don't need guns to stop a rapist on campus:

> It's why we have call boxes, it's why we have safe zones, it's why we have the whistles. Because you just don't know who you're gonna be shooting at. And you don't know if you feel like you're gonna be raped, or if you feel like someone's been following you around or if you feel like you're in trouble and when you may actually not be, that you pop out that gun and you pop—pop a round at somebody?

Amanda Collins, whom I spoke with recently on my television program, begs to differ. Collins, who had a concealed-carry license but was not permitted to carry her gun while on campus, was brutally raped inside a parking garage, less than one hundred feet from campus authorities.

"I was denied the one equalizing factor that I had," she said.

And what about those campus safe zones that Representative Salazar talked about? "Well," Collins said, "I was in a safe zone and my attacker didn't care."

Gun-free zones don't deter criminals—they help them by providing a guarantee that they will not face any armed resistance. But they do deter the law-abiding. A faculty member with a concealed-handgun permit who breaks the campus gun ban would be fired and likely find it impossible to get hired at another university. A student with a permit who brings a gun to school faces expulsion and would probably find it difficult to get admitted to another school. Bringing a firearm into a gun-free zone can have serious adverse consequences for law-abiding people. But for someone like the Virginia Tech killer, the threat of expulsion is no deterrent at all.

THE POLICE SUPPORT MORE GUN CONTROL LAWS—YOU SHOULD, TOO.

"I don't understand why the police officers across this country don't stand up collectively and say we're going to go on strike [until more gun control is adopted]."
—*MAYOR MICHAEL BLOOMBERG*, July 23, 2012

It is illegal for police to go on strike, and Bloomberg later backed off his statement. But, aside from the fact that he probably should've known that already, this is a classic case of once again trying to click those heels and wish that people would behave the way you think they should. However, unlike with his restrictions on cigarettes, painkillers, and baby formula, Bloomberg can't just force the police into believing that more gun control is needed.

The annual survey by the National Association of Chiefs of Police polls more than twenty thousand chiefs of police and sheriffs. In 2010, 95 percent of respondents said they believed that "any law-abiding citizen [should] be able to purchase a firearm for sport or self-defense." Seventy-seven percent said that concealed-handgun permits issued in one state should be honored by other states "in the way that drivers' licenses are recognized through the country" and that making citizens' permits portable would "facilitate the violent-crime-fighting potential of the professional law enforcement community."

National surveys of street officers are rare, but the ones that have been done show officers to be overwhelmingly in favor of law-abiding civilians' owning and carrying guns. A 2007 national survey of sworn police officers by *Police* magazine found that 88 percent did not agree that "tighter restrictions on handgun ownership would increase or enhance public safety." In the same survey, 67 percent said they opposed tighter gun control because the "law would only be obeyed by law-abiding citizens."

Regional and local surveys show similar patterns. For example, a 1997 survey conducted by the San Diego Police Officers Association found that 82 percent of its officers opposed an "assault weapons" ban, 82 percent opposed a limitation on magazine capacity, and 85 percent supported letting law-abiding private citizens carry concealed handguns. And, just recently, the nonpartisan association that represents all 62 of Colorado's elected sheriffs issued a position paper against attempts to limit the capacity of magazines. "Law enforcement officers carry high-capacity magazines because there are times when 10 rounds might not be enough to end the threat," the group wrote. "County Sheriffs of Colorado believe the same should hold true for civilians who wish to defend themselves, especially if attacked by multiple assailants."

So, Mr. Mayor, maybe the reason police aren't begging for more gun control is the very same one that, despite the evidence, you won't listen to: our cops know that more guns mean less crime.

WE SHOULD RESTRICT MAGAZINES TO A MAXIMUM OF TEN ROUNDS.

"[W]hy can't we restrict the big magazines? If you sort of have a smaller magazine, it's very likely fewer people would have gotten shot in Tucson. Why can't we ban assault weapons?"

—*E. J. DIONNE JR.* (Washington Post *columnist*), January 13, 2011

"Extended magazines for handguns, for example, are not used in hunting. They're not used in self-defense. An extended magazine for a handgun is the sort of thing that is only used for killing a large number of humans or trying to."
—*RACHEL MADDOW, January 10, 2011*

"What we're trying to do, which seems reasonable, is to limit the number of rounds in a magazine to two. Excuse me, to 10. That was in the Assault Weapons Ban, which we allowed to expire. At least 10 fewer people would had been shot [in Tucson] had that been the case and I can't understand any rational argument for not, at least restricting the size of the magazines to 10."
—*REPRESENTATIVE JIM MORAN (D-VA), January 13, 2011*

This is such common sense that I can't believe we haven't done it already! Just limit the number of bullets a magazine can hold to ten and mass killings will magically disappear. Or should it be seven bullets, as New York has decided? Or five? Or, as Senator Feinstein suggested many years ago, three rounds?

Or how about zero?

A magazine is basically a metal or plastic box with a spring. Before 3-D printing came into existence it was pretty easy for people to make these at home. A few years from now, anyone will be able to make a magazine in virtually any size they want. Restricting their capacity to some arbitrary number may ensure that law-abiding people can't buy a larger one, but it will not stop a criminal who wants one, especially since many millions are already in circulation.

In some ways I can understand this argument, since it follows the typical pattern. Controllists think more guns mean more crime, so naturally they think more ammunition means more fatalities from mass killings. The problem is that the data just doesn't bear that out.

Mother Jones, whose data issues we've already covered, claims that half of the incidents they looked at involved magazines holding more than ten bullets. That's thirty-one incidents over the last thirty years. Whether U.S. policy involving millions of people, not to mention a constitutional right, should really be changed over something that happens an average of once a year can be debated—but let's put that aside and instead think about the practical impact on criminals of restricting magazine sizes.

I looked at the underlying *Mothers Jones* data from those thirty-one incidents involving so-called high-capacity magazines (remember, a 30-round magazine is *standard* on many guns) and found that twenty of them involved a killer who brought multiple guns to the scene. Using multiple weapons is obviously one convenient way around any kind of magazine capacity restriction. (Having multiple smaller magazines is another way around it, but then you get into dumb arguments about how quickly someone can switch magazines.) If you exclude the massacres where the murderer possessed multiple firearms, you are left with eleven incidents. Over three decades.

Controllists like to make the argument that a gunman who has to reload is more likely to be stopped during that process, but I know of only two incidents where that has ever actually happened: Tucson and the 1993 Long Island Rail Road massacre. If others exist I'd be curious to know why those who think that restricting magazine size will reduce fatalities do not cite them more often.

There is also the obvious issue of control. Once a magazine limit is determined, controllists have a starting point. Right now they are fighting for ten, but is that really the end of it? In his essay *Guns,* Stephen King gave a glimpse into how this mentality works: "Ban the sale of clips and magazines containing more than ten rounds. I think that's too many; to borrow the title of an old sitcom, I believe eight is enough. But I'd happily accept ten."

So he'd happily accept ten . . . right now. But what about a few years from now? Will he push for eight? You can see how quickly this can get out of hand. In fact, controllists may have found a back door into the overall gun ban they dream of. After all, the Constitution may guarantee the right to keep and bear arms, but it says nothing about ammunition.

Many gun control advocates don't care about the data or the practicality or the history (or the Constitution) and instead simply can't stand the idea that these magazines even exist. *Why does anyone need a thirty-round magazine,* they ask rhetorically.

I think there are two answers. The first is simple: none of your business. We are not a "needs-based" society when it comes to rights. We don't dole out freedoms based on the collective wisdom of some group of elitists. The second reason is more practical, though controllists aren't going to like it: sometimes people need more than seven or ten bullets to defend themselves.

There are plenty of examples to highlight, but a recent one occurred in late February 2013 in Houston. A family was baking a cake in their kitchen when three men invaded their home. After taking down the father the men went for his wife. Their son, seeing what was happening, ran and got his father's gun. He opened fire, killing one of the attackers and forcing the others to flee. Had his gun started clicking after seven or ten shots this home invasion could have ended very differently.

Controllists may scoff, but it's a pretty good bet that the number of lives saved each year because law-abiding people had access to magazines holding more than ten rounds is greater than the lives lost in mass killings because the gunmen did. For some reason, that other side is never counted—maybe because stories about people saving their own lives are not as interesting to the media as those where lives are taken.

One final note on this topic. There's a fairly widespread belief among those who have probably never held a gun before that so-called assault weapons hold larger magazines than hunting rifles. But that is totally wrong. *Any* gun that can hold a magazine can hold one of virtually any size. And that is true for handguns as well as rifles. An "assault weapon" ban would therefore not limit the number of rounds that guns could fire.

▌ DON'T BELIEVE THE GUN NUTS: HITLER DIDN'T ▌ TAKE ANYONE'S FIREARMS AWAY.

"Gun control in Germany came prior to Hitler, and Hitler in fact relaxed gun control laws (though not for the Jews and other groups)."
—DAILY KOS

"By 1938, when Hitler was riding high, those laws were pretty much the same as American gun laws today . . . you needed a permit to acquire and carry a handgun, but you could have as many rifles as you wanted. Unless you were a Jew, of course, but that was the annoying thing about the Nazis, wasn't it? They killed lots of Jews, and they didn't need restrictive gun legislation to do it; it was the government that armed the killers."
—*STEPHEN KING*, Guns

One of the ways that dictatorships maintain their power is by disarming opponents in order to prevent resistance. Tyrants no more recognize the right to keep and bear arms than they do the right to free speech. Yet, for some reason, people are either confused or in denial about how this worked in regard to Nazi Germany.

Some claim that Hitler and the Nazis didn't disarm people because gun control laws were already in place before he rose to power. This is partially true—as I'll detail later on—but first I have a much more important question: so what?

If there had been no gun control laws in Germany prior to Hitler, and the German people were as heavily armed as Americans are today, would things still have played out the same way?

Obviously, no one knows for sure—but it's hard to make a convincing case that things could've been much worse.

Let's put the hypotheticals aside for now and instead go through the actual history to see how gun control and confiscation really worked. Once you have the facts and understand the time line it'll be a lot easier to see how important gun control was for the Nazis.

Before Hitler rose to power, it was the Weimar Republic's gun laws of 1928 and 1931 that ruled the land. They provided that "licenses to obtain or to carry firearms shall only be issued to persons whose reliability is not in doubt, and only after proving a need for them." It also prohibited gun possession for anyone "who has acted in an inimical manner toward the state, or it is to be feared that he will endanger the public security."

A 1931 Weimar "emergency decree" authorized the German states to register all firearms, which could be confiscated if "public security and order so requires." The interior minister warned the states to provide "the secure storage of the lists of persons who have registered their weapons," so that they would not "fall into the hands of radical elements." Unfortunately, they never considered that those radical elements might be the government itself and those lists would eventually fall right into the hands of the Nazis.

According to Stephen P. Halbrook, a constitutional attorney who has done extensive research on German firearm laws, "the Nazi seizure of power in 1933 was consolidated by massive searches and seizures of firearms from political opponents, who were invariably described as 'communists.' "

After Hitler became chancellor in 1933, the Nazis used gun control to repress Jews and political opponents. Using the Reichstag (the German parliament building) fire as evidence of an impending plot to overthrow the government, Hitler successfully pushed through the ironically titled "Decree of the Reich President for the Protection of People and State" emergency measure. This decree suspended civil liberties, thereby allowing the state to restrict basic rights, like freedom of the press, freedom of speech, and freedom of assembly. Guarantees of personal privacy were also suspended as Nazi police began to search homes and offices for subversive literature and firearms under the guise of suppressing "Communists."

During the early months of 1933, storm troopers raided the apartment of the widow of Friedrich Ebert, the first president of the Weimar Republic. According to the *New York Times,* they searched "for hidden arms, but found only a revolver belonging to Herr Ebert [Jr.], which he handed to them together with a permit that had expired."

A few days later, perhaps to send a message that no one was immune, they searched the home of another notable person: Albert Einstein. The *Times* reported: "Charging that Professor Albert Einstein had a huge quantity of arms and ammunition stored in his secluded home in Caputh, the National Socialists sent Brown Shirt men and policemen to search it today, but the nearest thing to arms they found was a bread knife."

That might be embarrassing to some governments, but it did not slow the Nazis down. The following month, Nazi police conducted several mass searches throughout Germany. The *Times* reported:

> A large force of police assisted by Nazi auxiliaries raided a Jewish quarter in Eastern Berlin, searching everywhere for weapons and papers. Streets were closed and pedestrians were halted. Worshipers leaving synagogues were searched and those not carrying double identification cards were arrested. Even flower boxes were overturned in the search through houses and some printed matter and a few weapons were seized.

One week later, the *Times* reported that Nazi police had searched passengers' baggage at railway stations: "Truckloads of trunks filled with Communist literature, arms and munitions were seized in Berlin and other cities."

As the home inspections and mass searches continued, Nazi authorities turned their attention to the licensing and registration records they had on gun owners thanks to the original Weimar law. In April 1933, the *Times* reported the following from Breslau:

> The Police President of the city has decreed that "all persons now or formerly of the Jewish faith who hold permits to carry arms or shooting licenses must surrender them forthwith to the police authorities."
>
> The order is justified officially on the grounds that Jewish citizens have allegedly used their weapons for unlawful attacks on members of the Nazi organization and the police.
>
> Inasmuch as the Jewish population "cannot be regarded as trustworthy," it is stated, permits to carry arms will not in the future be issued to any member thereof.

This confiscation was permissible based on the Weimar firearms law, still in effect, which authorized the disarming of persons deemed dangerous to public safety. Police had discretion to cancel firearm permits at will.

The next five years (1933–38) saw National Socialism imposed on all aspects of society, including a planned economy, work camps for dissidents, racial purity laws, the elimination of Jews from professions, and the forcing into line of labor, sports, and culture through both propaganda and coercion.

In 1938, Hitler revised the Weimar law to exclude Jews from firearms businesses, ban .22-caliber hollow-point bullets, and stipulate that anyone could be disarmed on "public security" grounds. At the same time, some provisions for "loyal" Germans were softened. For example, an acquisition license was no longer required for long guns, so long as the state determined that you were not a threat.

In November 1938, using the homicide of an official at the German embassy in Paris by a Jewish teenager from Poland as the impetus, and relying on those helpful Weimar firearm registration lists, the Nazis disarmed Jews all over Germany during what's now called Kristallnacht, the "Night of Broken Glass." Jewish homes and shops were ransacked and synagogues were burned. Thousands of Jewish men were thrown into concentration camps.

On November 9, 1938, under the headline BERLIN POLICE HEAD ANNOUNCES "DISARMING" OF JEWS, the *Times* reported:

> The Berlin Police President, Count Wolf Heinrich von Helldorf, announced that as a result of a police activity in the last few weeks the entire Jewish population of Berlin had been "disarmed" with the confiscation of 2,569 hand weapons, 1,702 firearms and 20,000 rounds of ammunition. Any Jews still found in possession of weapons without valid licenses are threatened with the severest punishment.

It's interesting to note that the Jews were already being disarmed weeks before the German embassy killing in Paris (the incident that supposedly necessitated the confiscation). That means the raids had been planned well in advance. I guess the saying "Never let a serious crisis go to waste" wasn't invented yesterday.

A couple of days later, on November 11, 1938, the *New York Times* published an article headlined POSSESSION OF WEAPONS BARRED, which reported on the confiscation of weapons from the Jews:

One of the first legal measures issued was an order by Heinrich Himmler, commander of all German police, forbidding Jews to possess any weapons whatever and imposing a penalty of twenty years confinement in a concentration camp upon every Jew found in possession of a weapon hereafter.

It's pretty incredible that those who talk about guns and Nazis usually treat the disarmament of the Jews as though it's a minor point. The *Daily Kos* article quoted above puts this fact in parentheses, saying "Hitler in fact relaxed gun control laws (though not for the Jews and other groups)" as though it's almost an afterthought. Stephen King references it only so that he can make an idiotic point that, since it was the government that did the killing, the fact that the Jews lost their guns made no difference.

Disarming the people most likely to stand up to you (and using registration lists to do it) is not an afterthought at all—it's the whole point! Could the German Jews single-handedly have defeated the Nazis? No—absolutely not. But could they have mounted a much stronger resistance, or put up enough of a fight to encourage their countrymen or other nations to join them? We'll never know.

Finally, there's a legitimate question to be asked about whether loyal, Christian Germans were really allowed to purchase and keep firearms—even if they followed the restrictive rules. In 1940, the *New York Times* published an article that related the conditions in France after the Nazi occupation to the way the German people had lived for years:

The best way to sum up the disciplinary laws imposed upon France by the German conqueror is to say that the Nazi decrees reduce the French people to as low a condition as that occupied by the German people. Military orders now forbid the

French to do things which the German people have not been allowed to do since Hitler came to power. To own radio senders or to listen to foreign broadcasts, to organize public meetings and distribute pamphlets, to disseminate anti-German news in any form, *to retain possession of firearms—all these things are prohibited for the subjugated people of France, as they have been verboten these half dozen years to the people of Germany.* (emphasis added)

The facts are clear to anyone willing to see them: Hitler used existing gun control laws to consolidate power and then he confiscated firearms from Jews and other opponents to ensure he would keep it. It was a key part of his ability to extinguish any flicker of hope by the opposition and it's why, in the midst of World War II, he was quoted during his "Table Talk" monologues as saying:

> The most foolish mistake we could possibly make would be to allow the subject races to possess arms. History shows that all conquerors who have allowed their subject races to carry arms have prepared their own downfall by so doing.

I'm pretty sure I've ever said this before, but, in this case, Hitler was right. Those who would prefer to rewrite history so that it better fits their current political agenda would be smart to read his actual words and open their eyes to what really happened. The reason that history so often repeats is not only human nature, but also human ignorance.

PART TWO

Winning Hearts and Minds

Adam Smith's most famous book is *The Wealth of Nations,* but his more important work came seven years earlier, when he wrote *The Theory of Moral Sentiments.* While most people have never heard of that book, it was the key to everything. Smith realized that the free market could never work unless people first understood morality and human nature. When a breakdown in the free market occurs, it's not the market's fault; it's the fault of individual participants who've lost their way.

The same principle holds true for guns. The Second Amendment, like all of our rights, is reliant on a moral and virtuous people. Without that, nothing else matters. Man cannot rule himself if, as Smith put it, moral sentiment is missing.

That, I contend, is the answer. Not just to gun violence, but to many of the other problems that plague us. We must stop looking to assign blame to the choices we are offered—whether it's guns or large sodas or tanning beds—and instead take personal responsibility for our choice and our lives. It's clear to me that if we raise children with no moral compass, we are planting the seeds of our own destruction. As Benjamin Franklin once wrote, "[O]nly a virtuous people are capable of freedom. As nations become corrupt and vicious, they have more need of masters."

But the good news is that the opposite also holds true: if we can restore morality and responsibility and virtue back to their rightful places, we are planting the seeds of a future filled with hope and opportunity.

It is my hope that now, after showing that guns are not the problem, this section will prove what really is.

* * *

To claim that America's "culture of violence" is responsible for school shootings is tantamount to cigarette company executives declaring that environmental pollution is the chief cause of lung cancer.

—STEPHEN KING, *Guns*

At 7:45 a.m. on a frosty Monday in December 1997, a bespectacled fourteen-year-old boy walked into his Kentucky high school and made his way toward the lobby outside the principal's office. There, an informal group of thirty-five to forty kids stood in a large circle saying their morning prayers. The boy, a freshman who played baritone saxophone in the high school band, waited for the final "Amen" before taking a stolen handgun out of his backpack and opening fire.

By most accounts, the boy fired eight to ten shots into the group. By the time he put his weapon down three of his classmates were dead and five more had been wounded. Before the police arrived, the boy spoke to his principal and seemingly could not believe what he'd just done. "It was kind of like I was in a dream," he said. "And then I woke up."

As the reality began to settle in, the boy looked up at his friend who had come to stand by his side and said, "Kill me, please."

Investigators were stunned by the lethal accuracy in which the boy had carried out the massacre. Of the approximately eight shots he'd taken, he had registered eight hits. That's pretty remarkable for two reasons: First, the FBI reports that, in shoot-out scenarios, experienced officers register a hit with only 20 percent of their shots from seven yards. Second, before stealing the gun, and firing two clips of ammo the night before the massacre, this ninth-grade boy had never fired a real pistol.

During the investigation, police learned that the boy had honed his shooting skills by playing hundreds of hours of video games. The incident itself had apparently been modeled after a similar scene in the movie *Basketball Diaries*. And one other thing: the boy's locker contained a book about a student who brings a gun to school, kills his teacher, and holds his class hostage.

The book? *Rage*, by Stephen King.

* * *

I want to get a few major disclaimers out of the way right up front so that there's no confusion:

I don't believe that violent video games can turn a normal kid into a cold-blooded killer.

I don't believe that watching violent TV shows can take a kid who loves his life and respects his family and turn him into a monster.

I don't believe that violent movies or music videos or rap songs can force kids to massacre their classmates.

Because I don't believe any of that, I also don't think the answer is to ban video games or television shows or movies.

I believe in the First Amendment just as much as the Second; I believe in more speech, not less. I don't want to write more laws or pass more regulations or give some government agency more oversight.

I believe in more freedom, not less.

I have a lot of ideas for how we can fix this, but none of them involves the Federal Trade Commission or the ATF or the hallowed halls of Congress.

I do, however, believe passionately in personal responsibility. I believe that all of us, as parents, brothers, sisters, coworkers, and mentors, have a role to play in our communities.

I believe that, with a few obvious exceptions, we all know right from wrong and good from evil. Or—at least I used to believe that. With all that is happening in the world lately, I'm not so sure anymore. We are all born with common sense, but we don't all use it. Many people have seemingly decided that the easy answer is always the right one. We put our kids in front of video games and iPads and then we get hostile when someone dares to say that maybe that's not the best thing for their developing brains. Instead of taking responsibility we blame the messenger.

With all of that being said, and with all due respect to Stephen King (he's a wonderful writer of fiction, after all), his analogy about cigarettes and lung cancer only hurts his argument. While there's great evidence to suggest that cigarettes are a major contributing factor to lung cancer, smokers who die of lung cancer have a very hard time proving to juries that cigarettes are specifically what killed them. Why? Well, one reason is because fewer than 10 percent of lifelong smokers will ever get lung cancer. Fewer still will die from it. It's virtually impossible to take a person with lung cancer and isolate the effects that his smoking had from the effects of everything else he did in his life—even if it's clear that cigarettes were the primary risk factor.

To make the direct connection—and control for all other variables—researchers would need to design a controlled, double-blind study like the ones used by the Food and Drug Administration in considering new prescription drugs. But, at least here in

America, we don't commission studies where the primary objective is getting lung cancer. We don't use "placebo cigarettes" to measure one group against another. As a result, we don't know, with absolute scientific certainty, that smoking cigarettes directly causes lung cancer.

Yet, even without that absolute certainty, we've tightly regulated tobacco companies to the point where massive warnings and disgusting photos of disease-ridden organs are printed directly onto their product as a way to discourage use. Why? Because society has basically accepted that the link between cigarettes and cancer exists, even if researchers aren't able to design a study that scientifically proves it.

And that brings us back to Stephen King.

Just as with cigarettes and cancer, it will *never* be scientifically possible to prove that consuming violent entertainment results in an increased propensity for violence. We can listen to what the killers themselves say and we can look at the statistics and studies that show the strong correlation, but we will never be able to design a study that would prove it conclusively. Why? Well, think about what that study would have to look like:

1. First, we'd have to select a large group of kids of similar demographics and upbringings.
2. Next, those children would have to live in a lab environment controlled by the researchers for a significant amount of time. Everything these kids do would need to be monitored and controlled: what they eat; what they do for fun; what they learn in school; how their parents raise and discipline them. Remember, the idea is to isolate violent-media consumption as the *only* factor having an impact on their lives.
3. During the study we'd have to force half of the kids to play violent games and watch violent television for three or four

      hours a day while the other half read poetry or listened to
      Michael Bolton songs.

  4. For the next forty or fifty years we'd have to individually track
      each of the kids to see what happens in their lives.

Unfortunately, even that study would fail, because as soon as the kids left the lab they'd be open to all kinds of outside influences. What if a child from the video game group later goes on a killing spree, but we subsequently find out that he'd been on all kinds of prescription drugs? What if a child from the control group kills his classmates but we later find out that he'd been traumatized after the study was done by seeing his father killed in a home invasion? How would these crimes be classified?

The issue is just not as simple as people would like it to be. When the *New York Times* asked Michael Ward, an economist at the University of Texas at Arlington who is studying the issue, whether violent video games increase the likelihood that someone will commit a violent crime later in life, he answered, "I don't know that a psychological study can ever answer that question definitively."

And that's the point: it will never be possible to scientifically prove this correlation. There are just too many variables, too many ways that even the best-designed studies can be corrupted. But that doesn't mean we simply dismiss the idea or stop looking for answers (even though that's what many people in the entertainment industry would like). In fact, just the opposite is true—we should be ramping up our efforts to understand this relationship.

Besides, data is only one part of the equation. The other part, common sense, is equally important—and, in this case, even more conclusive. Anyone who is willing to take the time to actually read about the video games our kids are playing (or better yet, to play those games themselves) will probably be shocked. I know I was.

Once I saw these games with my own eyes I was left with no doubt they should be classified as a risk factor. Just as good parents don't leave their children with unfettered access to pornography, good parents would never let their kid play a game where the goal is to commit increasingly heinous violent acts so you can move up the ranks of a criminal organization.

It does not mean, of course, that everyone who plays a game like *Grand Theft Auto* will become a spree killer, just as 90 percent of lifelong smokers will never get lung cancer. Unfortunately, this has become one of the most effective excuses of those who defend the industry. "I played all of those games and I've never killed anyone," they say.

That, of course, is true: most people who play violent games or watch violent TV *don't* commit violent acts. But that's not the way reasonable people look at an issue. Most people who fly in airplanes never die—but that doesn't mean we stop trying to improve aviation safety or never explore the causes of the rare accidents that do occur.

Lieutenant Colonel Dave Grossman, author of *Stop Teaching Our Kids to Kill,* is one of our country's foremost experts on the psychological aspects of killing. I asked Dave for his help with this part of the book because he's spent virtually his entire career, from being an Army Ranger to teaching psychology at West Point to traveling the country to train local law enforcement, on the subject of "killology"—the science of killing. After years of research and untold hours of field investigations—talking with killers and their friends and families—Grossman believes without a shadow of a doubt that we are literally training our children to be killers in the same way that armies train their soldiers.

Dave has a pretty compelling answer to the argument that most kids don't turn into killers—one that shows the idiocy of it. He tells people: "I never buckled my seat belt as a kid, and I'm just fine. None of my friends growing up used their seat belts, either, and none of them were killed in car accidents, either. Given all that evidence, why should I buckle my kids up?"

A surgeon general's report from the 1970s summarizes this point pretty well:

> [U]nder certain circumstances television violence can instigate an increase in aggressive acts. The accumulated evidence, however, does not warrant the conclusion that it has . . . an adverse effect on the majority of children. . . . The evidence does indicate that televised violence may lead to increased aggressive behavior in certain subgroups of children, who might constitute a small portion or a substantial proportion of the total population of young television viewers.

To say that violent media consumption is not a risk factor for violent aggression later in life means that you are either ignorant, have a political agenda, or, like Stephen King, are looking for some way to make yourself feel better about your contributions to the crisis.

U.S. Mass Killers and Violent Video Games

Below is a partial list of mass killers who have been influenced by violent video games. Although there are many more reported incidents, only those where the reports came from either the police or the killers themselves are included.

Newtown: According to CBS News, the killer was "motivated by violent video games." John Miller, a former FBI assistant director, said the gunman had a blacked-out gaming room where he immersed himself in the virtual reality of video games. "The only reality in that room," Miller told CBS, citing law enforcement sources, "was him and that TV screen with his tactical shooting game." Other reports have revealed that the killer allegedly spent years creating an incredibly detailed spreadsheet of previous massacres before the attack. According to a law enforcement source who spoke to the *New York Daily News*, "They [Connecticut State Police] don't believe this was just a spreadsheet. They believe it was a score sheet. This was the work of a video gamer, and that it was his intent to put his own name at the very top of that list. . . . It's why he didn't want to be killed by law enforcement. In the code of a gamer, even a deranged gamer like this little bastard, if somebody else kills you, they get your points. They believe that's why he killed himself.

The source, who was speaking after hearing a presentation from a Connecticut State Trooper at a law enforcement conference in March 2013, continued: "The fascination he had with this subject matter, the complete and total concentration. . . . There really was no other subject matter inside his head. Just this: Kill, kill, kill.

"It really was like he was lost in one of his own sick games. That's what we heard. That he learned something from his game that you learn in [police] school, about how if you're moving from room to room—the way he was in that school—you have to reload before you get to the next room. . . . They believe he learned the principles of this—the tactical reload—from his game. Reload before you're completely out. Keep going. When the strap broke on his first weapon, he went to his handgun at the end. Classic police training. Or something you learn playing kill games."

Columbine: According to *Newsweek*, "The two [killers] became 'obsessed' with the violent videogame *Doom*—an interactive game in which the players try to rack up the most kills—and played it every afternoon." One of the killers wrote, "*Doom* is so burned into my head my thoughts usually have something to do with the game. Whether it be a level or environment or whatever. . . . What I can't do in my real life, I try to do in *Doom*, like if I walk by a small building I would re-create it as good as I could and then explore it. Go on the roof, under it, or even shoot at it. The fact is, I love that game and if others tell me 'hey its just a game' I say 'I don't care.' "

Tucson: The man who tried to assassinate Congresswoman Gabby Giffords (and killed six others) is reported to have spent most of his time playing video games. And he posted a series of disturbing comments on gaming sites throughout the year before the massacre. One post read: "I bet your hungry. . . . Because i know how to cut a body open and eat you for more then a week. ;-)"

Paducah, Kentucky: The boy who killed three and wounded five of his fellow students told a psychiatrist that he liked to play *Quake* and *Doom*—two violent video games.

Fayette, Alabama: A teenager killed two police officers and a dispatcher after being brought into the station on suspicion that he'd stolen a car. After he was captured he reportedly told police, "Life is like a video game. Everybody's got to die sometime." Many have blamed the boy's obsession with the game *Grand Theft Auto* for his actions, as he appeared to have reenacted a scene from the game.

Interstate 40: In Tennessee two stepbrothers took rifles from their home, hid behind trees along the highway, and opened fire, killing one person and seriously wounding another. They told police they were trying to "re-create scenes from the cult game [*Grand Theft Auto*]."

Bull Run Middle School: A boy came to his school in Prince William County, Virginia, with a knife, butane fuel, a rifle, and one hundred rounds of ammunition. Fortunately, while he was loading his gun in the bathroom, someone recognized the sound and the boy was stopped before anyone was hurt. After searching the boy's home police found 13 different violent video games. His father said, "He played them too much, I am embarrassed to say."

Something Is Different

Before we get to the data, let's first take a closer look at the commonsense side of the equation.

Guns have always been around. In the 1700s, colonial Americans "were the most heavily armed people in the world" but homicides involving guns were "rare." From the early 1970s through the late '90s "the number of handguns owned by Americans increased 160 percent. . . . Yet over that period, the murder rate declined 27.7 percent."

Up until 1968, there was no federal law to prevent any child from walking into a hardware store and buying a high-capacity semi-auto pistol (say, a Browning Hi-Power with a high-capacity magazine, first marketed in 1935), or buying a high-capacity military rifle (maybe a World War II–era M-1 carbine, complete with thirty-round magazines), or buying a semi-automatic shotgun (perhaps a Browning Auto-5, first manufactured in 1905), and buying as much ammunition as they could afford.

Availability of "assault" weapons was not a problem in the 1940s, '50s, or most of the '60s . . . yet, for some reason, no juvenile had *ever* committed a multiple homicide in a school until 1975, when a sixteen-year-old shot and killed a student and teacher in Brampton, Canada (yes, it happened first in Canada). Four years later the United States experienced its first double homicide in a school when another sixteen-year-old killed two and injured nine more at a school across the street from her house in California.

Think about that. Five thousand years of recorded history. Five hundred years of gunpowder combat. One hundred and fifty years of repeating firearms. Yet, despite it all, no one can find a single case, anywhere in the world, where a juvenile committed a multiple homicide in a school prior to 1975.

Common sense tells us that maybe this isn't about the gun after all. Maybe it's about the person who's holding it.

That means we have an issue with our society and with our families and our schools. We have issues with parenting and mentoring and bullying and the way we treat depression and anxiety. We have an issue with kids' finding pleasure and solace by playing video games in darkened bedrooms and basements instead of running around outside with friends. We have an issue with kids' spending hours on their phones and computers texting and posting on Facebook instead of having real, personal connections and conversations with others. We have an issue with kids' having unfettered access to the worst the Internet has to offer instead of the best that our communities can provide.

We have a lot of new issues in America, but access to guns isn't one of them.

In 1999, *New York Times* columnist Maureen Dowd made a claim about those who talk about entertainment violence that is still heard today. "Blaming Hollywood and the culture, the Republicans' tired ploy," she wrote, "is a glib solution anyway. It's much easier than doing the hard work of financing and mounting a campaign for meaningful gun legislation, which might take years."

In other words, Dowd believes that those who implicate entertainment violence are only looking for a scapegoat. But, just like Stephen King, she has it completely backward. The truth is that it is those who blame guns who are the ones looking for a scapegoat. It is always much easier to look at "how" violence is carried out (that is, with a gun) than to look at "why" violence is carried out. Yet, in almost all cases *besides* those involving guns, that's exactly what we do: We look at *why*.

After 9/11, for example, people didn't take to the media to propose banning planes or tall buildings, but there were plenty of people advocating that we had to figure out *why* these young men became radicalized.

But that's not the way it seems to work with guns. We spend weeks talking about magazine clips and the definition of the term *semi-automatic* without ever really stopping to ask a simple question: *Why?*

A Worldwide Phenomenon

Despite what the media and most gun control advocates would like for you to believe, juvenile massacres are not just a new problem in America—they're happening around the world, even in places where gun access is significantly more restrictive.

In 2009, in Winnenden, Germany, a seventeen-year-old set a new mark for juvenile mass murderers when he killed fifteen people at his high school and during the subsequent chase and manhunt. The German media reported that he was an avid video game player.

Seven years earlier, in Erfurt, Germany, a nineteen-year-old expelled student murdered sixteen people in his former high school. The media reported that he too had "spent much of his time playing violent computer video games. His favorite was called *Counterstrike* in which anti-terror units wearing masks battle each other to the death."

Finland has also experienced this kind of violence. In 1989, a fourteen-year-old murdered two of his fellow students in his school in Rauma. Eight years later, in Tuusula, an eighteen-year-old student murdered eight classmates in his high school. The following year, a twenty-two-year-old student murdered ten people at Seinäjoki University.

Other countries have not been immune, either. In 2002, two people were murdered by a student at Monash University in Australia. Two more were murdered by a seventeen-year-old student in his school in Thailand in 2003. Four people were killed by a fifteen-year-old student in their Argentina high school in 2004, and thirteen were massacred in Brazil in 2011 when a former student returned to his old middle school with two .38-caliber revolvers. The list goes on and on.

Around the world, the generation that gave us these horrible crimes as juveniles in high school, and then as young adults in college, has grown up to give us even more horrific crimes as adults.

In 2011, a thirty-two-year-old man visited the Norwegian island of Utoya. There, in a place where his victims couldn't escape and not a single person could shoot back, he murdered sixty-nine people and injured at least 110—the vast majority of them teenagers at a summer camp. (He also killed eight people in Oslo earlier that day in a bombing.) This massacre was, far and away, the all-time worst solo act of gun violence in human history. Unsurprisingly, this killer also loved video games. In the year before the massacre, he would play *World of Warcraft* and *Call of Duty* extensively, sometimes up to sixteen hours a day.

Denying the Science

The vast majority of studies conclude that there is a cause-and-effect relationship between media violence and real-life violence. This link is undeniable and uncontestable.

—AMERICAN ACADEMY OF PEDIATRICS, 1995

Next time you go see a violent movie, take a moment before the previews start to look around the theater. How many young kids do you see? How many parents with toddlers or infants? How many middle school kids who snuck in?

What about television shows—do you let your kids watch prime-time TV? A 1998 study revealed that one-third of all American children ages two to eleven see the first hour of prime-time shows on weekday evenings. I think we can safely assume that percentage has only gotten higher in the fifteen years since.

If you successfully avoid movies and television, what about computers and tablets and phones? According to a report by Common Sense Media, American children under eight years old spend an average of two hours and fourteen minutes a day consuming digital media and television.

One of the most recent studies to be completed on entertainment violence was conducted by researchers at Brock University in Ontario and published in July 2012 in the journal *Developmental Psychology*. The goal was to determine if there was any correlation between the amount of time spent playing violent video games and the likelihood that a child (in this case 1,500 kids in grades nine through twelve) would exhibit aggressive behavior. Here's what the researchers found:

Sustained violent video game play was significantly related to steeper increases in adolescents' trajectory of aggressive behavior over time. Moreover, greater violent video game play predicted higher levels of aggression over time, after controlling for previous levels of aggression, supporting the socialization hypothesis.* In contrast, no support was found for the selection hypothesis. Nonviolent video game play also did not predict higher levels of aggressive behavior over time.

These results should not be a surprise, considering that they virtually mimic what has been found in other longitudinal studies (studies where researchers observe the same variables repeatedly over a long period of time) that were summarized by researchers in the book *Media Violence and Children:*

• 1963: 875 third graders in upstate New York were observed for twenty-two years and studied at two separate points in time. At the first study point, eleven years in, researchers "realized that TV viewing habits seemed to have played a substantial role in the development of aggression. In other words, the findings showed that exposure to TV violence during early childhood was predictive of higher levels of aggressive behavior at age 19."

Ten years later, researchers studied the group again and this time found that that "aggressive habits seemed to be learned early in life, and once established, are resistant to change and predictive of serious adult antisocial behavior. If a child's observation of media violence promotes the learning of aggressive habits, it can have harmful lifelong consequences." This study also revealed

---

* The "socialization hypothesis" is the theory that using violent video games predicts future aggressive behavior, while the "selection hypothesis" is the opposite: kids who are already aggressive seek out violent video games. This study found support only for the socialization hypothesis.

something even more shocking: TV viewing habits as a child was a predictor of violent criminal arrests at age thirty.

- 1981: Among 141 kindergartners in Connecticut, researchers found "a significant relationship between children's viewing of TV violence . . . and their aggressive behavior."

- 1984: Sixty-three kids, ages four to nine, were tracked for five years. Researchers found that "those who watched the most violent programming as preschoolers displayed the most aggression at age nine, even when controlling for initial levels of childhood aggression."

- 1986: One thousand kids from the United States, Israel, Finland, the Netherlands, Poland, and Australia were followed for three years. The report suggested that "early viewing of TV violence was significantly associated with higher levels of subsequent aggressive behavior, even after controlling for a child's initial level of aggressiveness." The only outlier country in this study was Australia.

The Verdict Is In

While nothing will ever be good enough for the Stephen Kings of the world, there have been thousands of studies performed and opinions issued over the last half century, many of which were highlighted in Grossman's book:

—1969: The National Commission on the Causes and Prevention of Violence cited *TV violence as a contributing factor to violence in our society.*

—1972: The surgeon general issued a report citing *a clear link between TV and movie violence, and aggressive behavior.*

—1975: The National Parent/Teacher Association (PTA) adopted a resolution demanding that networks and local

TV stations reduce the amount of violence in programs and commercials.

—1976: The American Medical Association adopted a resolution "to actively oppose TV programs containing violence, as well as products and/or services sponsoring such programs," in "recognition of *the fact that TV violence is a risk factor threatening the health and welfare of young Americans, indeed our future society.*"

—1982: The National Institute of Mental Health issued an extensive report stating that *there is clear consensus* on the strong link between TV violence and aggressive behavior.

—1984: The U.S. attorney general's Task Force on Family Violence stated that *the evidence is overwhelming* that TV violence contributes to real violence.

—1984: The American Academy of Pediatrics' Task Force on Children and Television cautioned physicians and parents that *TV violence promotes aggression.*

—1985: The American Psychological Association's Commission on Youth and Violence cited research showing a *clear link between TV violence and real violence.*

—1989: The National PTA again called for the TV industry to reduce the amount of violence in programs.

—1990: Congress passed the Television Violence Act, giving the three major networks an antitrust exemption so they could formulate a joint policy to reduce violence on TV.

—1992: The *Journal of the American Medical Association* published research concluding that "the introduction of television in the US in the 1950's caused a subsequent [15 years later] doubling of the homicide rate," and "if, hypothetically, TV technology had never been developed, there would today be 10,000 fewer murders each year in the US, 70,000 fewer rapes and 700,000 fewer injurious assaults."

—1992: An American Psychological Association report concluded that *forty years of research on the link between TV violence and real-life violence had been ignored.* They went on to state that the *"scientific debate is over"* and called for federal policy to protect society.

—1995: The American Academy of Pediatrics (a group that, by the way, is strongly in favor of significantly increasing gun control laws) stated that, "[a]lthough media violence is not the only cause of violence in American society, it is the single most easily remediable contributing factor."

—1998: UNESCO reviewed studies of media violence from twenty-five countries and documented an international concern that a *"global aggressive culture" is being formed by violent television and movies, particularly violent American TV shows and movies being exported around the world.*

The entertainment industry, along with people who prefer to blame guns for everything, like Stephen King and Maureen Dowd, wants to ignore this incredible body of scientific research. Through their lobbyists, they've spent vast sums of money on disinformation campaigns, and vicious, mocking rebuttals and attacks on every one of these scientific statements and the researchers behind them.

I know what it feels like to be attacked and smeared for standing up for what you believe in. But, for better or worse, giving my opinion is my chosen profession. That's not the case for these researchers and scientists. Most of them are not prepared for the onslaught to their reputations and careers that occurs when they put out studies that reveal the truth about entertainment violence. In many cases they eventually succumb to the pressure and move on to other, less controversial projects.

Stimulus/Response

The video game generation gave us Sandy Hook in elementary school, Jonesboro in middle school, Columbine in high school, and Virginia Tech in college. And, considering how rudimentary these video games are compared with what's to come, it will only get worse.

Those who've grown up being exposed to violence since the day they were born will eventually perpetrate massacres at our hospitals, our day-care centers, our Little League games, our churches, our school sporting events, and our school buses. There is no sacred place.

How do I know this? Because there's no other choice; this is the way we are raising them.

A study conducted by members of the Task Force on Television and Society appointed by the American Psychological Association revealed that the typical American youth had witnessed an average of 200,000 acts of violence on television by age eighteen. That's 200,000 acts of violence *just on television*. That doesn't include movies, video games, or the Internet. And that study was conducted in 1992, twenty years ago—does anyone really believe that entertainment has gotten *less* violent?

The other issue is how much time our kids spend watching this stuff. According to a study to be published in *Youth Violence and Juvenile Justice,* "It is estimated that children in the general population consume on average roughly 3 hours of electronic media, such as video games every day. . . . The estimate of daily electronic media consumption among youth in the psychiatric population is 6 hours per day."

As parents, we often try to make ourselves feel better by saying that children know the difference between real-world violence and what they see on TV. We try to convince ourselves that our child is too mature or too intelligent to be affected by it. But no matter how we try to justify it, it simply isn't true. According to the American Academy of Pediatrics, "At young ages (before age 8), children cannot uniformly discriminate between 'real life' and 'fantasy/entertainment.' They quickly learn that violence is an acceptable solution to resolving even complex problems, particularly if the aggressor is the hero."

Entertainment violence clearly teaches children the wrong life lessons, but it goes well beyond that: it actually affects the way their brains function. In a study published in the *Journal of Experimental Social Psychology,* participants played either a violent or nonviolent video game and were then shown violent and nonviolent photos while their brain activity was measured. Next, each participant played against an opponent in a game to measure their reaction time. They were told that whoever was slower in this game would receive an uncomfortable blast of white noise in their headphones. Each player was able to select the volume and length of the noise their opponent would receive. (In reality the "opponent" was only a computer, but participants did not know that.) The idea, of course, was to determine if those who'd played the violent games would be more aggressive with how much sound they blasted at their opponent.

The results were pretty remarkable:

> These data provide the first experimental evidence linking violence desensitization with increased aggression, and show that a neural marker of this process can at least partially account for the causal link between violent game exposure and aggression.
>
> [F]or individuals whose prior exposure to video game violence was low, playing a violent video game caused a reduction

in the brain's response to depictions of real-life violence, and
this reduction, in turn, predicted an increase in aggression.

The good news is that we may be able to flush out the hormones
that rush to children's brains while they are watching violent entertainment. Experts say that, while we need a lot more research,
current data indicates that we can "detox" a child in a couple of
days just by turning off the TV and video games.

But not all consequences can be so easily remedied; some have
much more long-lasting effects. A study conducted by researchers
at the Indiana University School of Medicine monitored the brain
function of young men before and after playing violent video
games. "For the first time," Dr. Yang Wang, an assistant research
professor in the IU Department of Radiology and Imaging Sciences, wrote, "we have found that a sample of randomly assigned
young adults showed less activation in certain frontal brain regions following a week of playing violent video games at home."

The regions of the brain that were found to be affected,
Dr. Wang continued, "are important for controlling emotion and
aggressive behavior." Unlike some hormones that can be flushed
out of the brain in a day or two, "These findings indicate that violent video game play has a long-term effect on brain functioning.
These effects may translate into behavioral changes over longer
periods of game play."

The Truth about (No) Consequences

I understand if all of these studies bore you; they kind of bore me,
too. But since the doubters always demand evidence, it's hard to win
this argument without having those kinds of facts on your side. But,
looking past all of the research, common sense alone tells us that
the kind of violence our children are witnessing is often far more

brutal than what most of us grew up with. *Pong* was the kind of game we remember from the 1970s. In the 1980s the most violent of the bestselling games was probably *Duck Hunt*—a game with crude graphics and a dog that laughed at you when you missed.

But today? Shooting games are no longer about hunting ducks; they're about hunting humans.

Consider Colonel Grossman's description of how the popular game *Duke Nukem* is played:

> [T]he shooter, who is controlled by the player and looks somewhat like the Terminator, moves through pornography shops, where he finds posters of scantily clad women he can use for target practice. In advanced levels, bonus points are awarded for the murder of female prostitutes, women who are usually naked. Duke often encounters defenseless, bound women, some of whom are even conveniently tied to columns and plead, "Kill me, kill me."

Manhunt, which has been a target of groups who've tried to get some games banned (and actually *was* banned in Australia), is especially gruesome. Josh Wanamaker, who writes for a website about video games, describes it like this:

> Players sneak around maze-like levels and were tasked with killing dudes in various gruesome ways, getting points for violence, essentially. Suffocating dudes with plastic bags, stabbing dudes in the face with knives, knocking dudes in the head with bats, sticking axes into dudes, etc. It's all really standard fare, actually. . . .

Grossman says that *Manhunt 2* is even worse.

> "Cave that man's head in with the baseball bat," the voice tells you. So you swing it really hard and "Boom!" your victim's head explodes.

"Ah that was good!" says the voice. "I didn't know you had it in you!"

"Take the knife and cut that woman's throat," the voice commands.

You hold the motion-capture device in your hand, and you sneak up behind your victim. When you move your hand, the knife and hand on the screen moves. You actually reach across and cut your victim's throat from ear to ear, and you watch her spin down, gurgling as blood gushes from her throat.

Introducing Your Child's Babysitter

Sometimes it takes reading descriptions of the games our kids are actually playing in order for parents to really connect with the magnitude of the problem. Here are a few of the worst, courtesy of Dave Grossman and Josh Wanamaker of Gameranx.com:

Grand Theft Auto: Grossman: "You play a criminal. You cannot be a 'good guy,' it is all about criminal behavior. These games are computer generated so you can play them for hundreds of hours without repeating yourself. And for hundreds of hours you steal enough stuff, you sell enough drugs, you kill enough cops, and you are going to make a lot of money.

"What do you do with all the money? One of the things you can do is to buy sex from a prostitute. Afterward, you can murder the woman you just had sex with, and get your money back. Screaming obscenities, in state-of-the-art graphic detail, you beat to death the woman you just had sex with, and you get your money back."

Postal 2: Wanamaker: "The game is nothing but a sandbox of senseless slaughter, hate, and pissing on people's heads. I'm not even kidding about that last part. Do you like the idea of running into a convenience store and screaming 'Rag Heads' whilst shooting up a bunch of Arabs? How about sticking a shotgun up a cat's anus to use the animal as a silencer?"

Grossman: "You kill every living creature in your town. You blow a girl's kneecap off with a sniper rifle. You blow a cop's leg off with sniper rifle. And then, as your victims writhe in agony you pour gasoline on them.

"It's 'you' doing this. You see your hands, you see the gas can, and you see your victims as you pour gasoline on them. Then, as your victims beg for mercy, you drop a match on them. 'Whoof!' they burst into flames. Their clothing and face char and burn in state-of-the-art detail as they scream in agony. But here is the big 'payoff' in the game. You urinate on your victims."

Soldier of Fortune: Wanamaker: "Shoot a dude in the stomach with a shotgun, out spill his intestines. Shoot a dude in the head, and depending on what part of the head you hit, a different part of the back of his skull would be blown out. Every part of a character model could be destroyed in hideous fashion, and while back then [2000] everyone was all 'WOW!' Today people would be more like 'meh.' Just . . . just don't let your kids play it, okay?"

Just so we are all clear on what depths of depravity these games are able to go to, none of the ones described here earned the highest rating a game can have of "Adults Only." Some of the worst games are available online and don't even need to be submitted to the Entertainment Software Rating Board (ESRB). For example, *V-Tech Rampage* and *Super Columbine Massacre RPG* are both online games that allow the player to be the killers in horrific real-life events and neither has an ESRB rating.

It's abundantly clear that entertainment violence fills kids' heads with the wrong kinds of images. But it does much more than that: it fills them with the wrong kinds of *messages.*

Think about the kinds of violence that are out there in popular culture. There is the gratuitous violence-for-violence's-sake, which is where I think many of the video games fit in. But there's also the superhero-beating-up-the-bad-guy-to-save-a-woman kind of violence—which is clearly preferable. And what about the consequences of violence? Does the perpetrator receive proper punishment or did it go unpunished, or was it even glorified?

Very often in video games you play a criminal and the crimes you commit are rewarded by gaining points and moving higher through the levels of the game. For the kids who play these games the criminals become the heroes and the cops become a force to be avoided or stopped in any way possible.

As parents we often unknowingly reinforce this sentiment. According to a study published in the journal *Youth Violence and Juvenile Justice,* "The consumption of violent media is far from innocuous, and when violent media consumption in the form of video games is viewed by adults as a 'reward' for youth to spend their free time, it can be problematic." Because we often allow our kids to play video games as a reward for good behavior, we are in effect telling them that we approve of the games and that the behavior they engage in while playing them is worthy of reward.

In addition to teaching children that violent and criminal behavior is what they should be striving toward, video games also have another big problem: they don't allow the players to "feel" anything. When the reality is virtual, players never experience any real consequences. There's no pain, no wounds or blood or agonizing trips to the ER.

Nonvirtual games, even those that could be considered violent, like paintball, teach that actions have consequences. Getting hit by a paintball hurts. A lot. Players quickly learn to treat the weapon with respect because they know what the pain feels like. The same principle is why law enforcement training usually entails the trainees' getting pepper sprayed and Tasered. We want these people to know what their weapons actually *feel* like when you're on the other end of them.

This is not the case with video games. The only consequence for dying in a game is having to press a button and start over again.

Trained to Kill

Soldiers who prepare for combat by using video game simulations often have very different reactions when they are first exposed to real-world violence. Evan Wright, the author of *Generation Kill: Devil Dogs, Iceman, Captain America, and the New Face of American War*, talked about his experience observing Marines in Iraq in 2003: "What I saw was a lot of [soldiers] discovered levels of innocence that they probably didn't think they had. When they actually shot people, especially innocent people, and were confronted with this, I saw guys break down. The violence in games hadn't prepared them for this."

The simulated violence in video games has two big problems: it desensitizes people, making it easier for them to commit acts of violence in the real world, and at the same time leaves these people unprepared for the consequences of that violence. According to Grossman, this claim about desensitization is something that the gaming industry has refuted over and over again, yet it's also something they eagerly advertise when it comes to the military.

How did video games and the military ever come to link up? Well, in World War II only 15–20 percent of individual riflemen fired their weapons in close combat. The problem was that these infantry had been trained by firing at standard bull's-eye targets. While this trained them to shoot accurately, it did a terrible job of preparing them to kill actual persons.

Our military has overcome this problem by using something called "operant conditioning." Now, instead of shooting at a bull's-eye, soldiers shoot at a man-shaped target that pops up. If they hit it, the target drops down, and once they hit a certain number of targets they're rewarded. This system was intentionally designed to apply B. F. Skinner's "operant conditioning" model, which many of us remember from the "rat lab" in Psych 101: stimulus, response; stimulus, response; until the behavior becomes automatic. Like a child in a fire drill at school, we have turned killing into a "conditioned response"—and it has worked. The firing rate went from 15 percent in World War II, to 55 percent in Korea, to upwards of 95 percent since Vietnam.

Today, this process has evolved into modern, highly realistic "combat simulators" that are now pretty much widespread throughout the military. Research from the Center for the Study of Violence, located at Iowa State University, suggested that "the U.S. Defense Department has spent $1 billion on games technology that gets soldiers combat ready." Sergeant Donel Hagelin, an Army "simulator facilitator," said that "combat simulators [are] . . . the fastest way to train troops and the easiest way to save money."

While the games used to train our soldiers are not the same ones you can go buy at your local store, they're not as far off as you might think. *Rainbow Six* is an off-the-shelf video game about a counterterrorism unit that has to plan out very specific missions in response to terrorist threats. It is such a successful and realistic game that, according to the book *Media Violence and Children,* "the U.S. Army has licensed the game engine to train their special operations soldiers. Furthermore, the U.S. Army has created their own violent video game as a recruitment tool."

According to Colonel Grossman, one of the Army's most widely used and effective simulators is called MACS, "the Multipurpose Arcade Combat Simulator." This tool, he says, is really "nothing more than a modified Super Nintendo game (except with a plastic M16 firing at typical military targets on a TV screen). It is an excellent, ubiquitous military marksmanship-training device."

Commonly available video games can perform the same function for children. Modern training for military and law enforcement teaches the two key components for successfully killing another human being: skill and will. These components are developed by putting trainees in highly realistic simulators where they can shoot at targets that represent what they may actually be called upon to kill someday. And that is exactly how some of the most violent video games work as well.

Remember the story earlier in the book about the Kentucky high school prayer group massacre? Many experts, including Colonel Grossman, were shocked at the killer's accuracy. According to a statement that Grossman made before the New York State legislature, "[A] 14-year old boy who had never fired a handgun before, stole a pistol, fired a few practice shots the night before and came into his school the next morning with the gun. In this case 8 shots were apparently fired, for 8 hits—4 of them head shots, one neck, and 3 upper torso. This is simply astounding [for an untrained gunman]."

The man responsible for the twin attacks in Norway (a bombing in Oslo and then a mass killing at a summer camp) that left seventy-seven dead is one of the most glaring examples of how these games can help make killers more deadly. At his trial the killer tried to make it clear that his video game addiction had no bearing on his rampage, but he also admitted that he used one game in particular as part of his training. According to the *New*

York Times, "[H]e spent four months through February 2010 playing . . . *Call of Duty: Modern Warfare,* for six hours a day. That game, he said, helped him hone his shooting skills because he was able to practice with the aid of its holographic sight. 'You could give the sight to your grandmother and she would become a supermarksman,' he said."

Grossman also pointed to the recent Los Angeles Jewish day-care center massacre as evidence of video game training: "[T]he shooter is reported to have fired 70 shots, and wounded 5 individuals. This is what should be expected from an untrained shooter." But this boy [in Paducah] was not untrained—he was an avid video game player. "[H]e 'stood still,' " Grossman said, "firing two-handed, not wavering far to the left or far to the right in his shooting 'field,' and firing only one shot at each target, [which] are all behaviors that are completely unnatural to either trained or 'native' shooters, behaviors that could only have been learned in a video game."

In addition to improving overall marksmanship, video games also teach children where they should aim to inflict maximum damage. Brad Bushman at Ohio State University recently published research demonstrating that video game players were able to pick up real guns and not only be more accurate than others, but also notch "99% more head shots." Bushman points out, "We didn't tell players to aim for the head—they did that naturally because the violent shooting game they played rewarded head shots."

The terms "natural" and "shoot a person in the face" do not go together. Humans aren't born with that instinct. In fact, only a very small percentage of murderers will shoot their victims in the face. The Newtown, Connecticut, killer, who reportedly shot his own mother several times in the head, was one of them.

Many top law enforcement agencies and departments also use

a video-game-based training device. FATS, the "Fire Arms Training Simulator," is, according to Grossman, similar to the violent video game *Time Crisis*. FATS helps trainees to feel the emotional response that comes from being in an extremely stressful and unpredictable situation.

The *New York Times* described one scenario from the game:

> [In] "Drunk Man With Baby," a weaving figure appears in an alley carrying an infant in a car seat. Within 10 seconds, he is already upon you, drawing a machete from the car seat. The man ignores all orders to stop and to place the baby on the ground. Then, with one hand, he suddenly lifts the machete to strike while holding tightly to the baby with the other. You have no choice but to shoot him and hope for the best.

That is not far off from many of the situations presented to kids who play a game like *Grand Theft Auto*, except, in the off-the-shelf version, kids play the criminal, not the hero.

The obvious question is why, if these kinds of games are good for our soldiers and police, they're not okay for our kids. Geoffrey Alpert, a professor of criminology at the University of South Carolina, explains: "Static target practice teaches you how to fire a gun, but it's not really relevant to the real world. You want officers in stressful situations to revert to their training, and unless you do scenario and role-play training, they're not going to have the experience to fall back on."

Our kids don't have that training and experience to fall back on. Members of our military and law enforcement are subject to an extremely high level of discipline and training. Appropriate use of weapons is ingrained in them. That's not the case with our kids. All they know is that violence is rewarded in the games and that their parents reward them by allowing them to play these games.

Rage

As I mentioned earlier, a copy of Stephen King's book *Rage*, which is about a troubled boy who brings a gun to school, kills his algebra teacher, and holds his class hostage, was found in the locker of the boy who committed the massacre at his Kentucky school. But, according to King himself, this boy was not the only one influenced by this book.

In 1988, in San Gabriel, California, a boy held fellow students hostage with a rifle until he was disarmed by a student and arrested. He reportedly told police that he got the idea from *Rage*. The following year, a boy in Jackson, Kentucky, held students in his school hostage with a revolver and a shotgun before eventually surrendering to police. The hostage negotiator later said it was as though he were acting out a scene from *Rage*, the book he'd been reading. In 1996, a boy in Moses Lake, Washington, killed his teacher and two students and then recited a quote from *Rage*. In a recent essay, King himself admitted that *Rage* was known to each of these killers.

In response, King had *Rage* pulled from store shelves and it hasn't been back in print yet. In explaining his decision he said that the book was a "possible accelerant" in each of these cases, but that we don't give these kids "blueprints to express their hate and fear. Charlie [the book's main character] had to go. He was dangerous." And yet, even after all of this, King still claims that he doesn't "believe the . . . assertion . . . that America's so-called culture of violence plays a significant role in kid-on-kid school shootings."

Do you think someone might be in a little bit of denial?

Scapegoating and Excuses

The people who blame guns for everything—I call them "controllists"—usually believe that those who bring up other issues, like entertainment violence, are simply trying to find a scapegoat. But I think this argument is completely backward. It's those who close their eyes as to *why* people pick up a gun in the first place who are scapegoating.

In his essay *Guns,* Stephen King wrote, "The assertion that Americans love violence and bathe in it daily is a self-serving lie promulgated by fundamentalist religious types and America's propaganda-savvy gun pimps." In order to back that up, he claims that some video game sales are slowing down and that "[i]n video gaming, shooters still top the lists, but sales of some, including the various iterations of *Grand Theft Auto* and *Call of Duty,* have softened by as much as 4 percent."

Stephen King may be a brilliant novelist, but he's a terrible financial analyst. Even if we take what he wrote at face value, which we shouldn't, it is still one of the most ridiculous excuses I've ever heard. To say that, *yeah, okay, violent shooting games are still the best-selling games in America, but some of them are down 4 percent!* shows just how far entertainment violence defenders are willing to go.

Since King brought up *Call of Duty,* let's take a look at some real numbers. In 2009, Activision, the company that publishes the game, reported that their *Call of Duty* franchise had grossed more than $3 billion in worldwide retail sales. "If you consider the number of hours our audiences are engaged in playing *Call of Duty* games," CEO Bobby Kotick wrote, "it is likely to be one of the most viewed of all entertainment experiences in modern history."

In November, 2010 *Call of Duty: Black* Ops took in an all-time record $360 million in its first twenty-four hours. It took just

forty-two days for the title to gross $1 billion. A newspaper esti-
mated that more than 600 million hours had been logged playing
the game in its first six weeks alone and Microsoft had disclosed
that their Xbox users log on more than once a day and play for
more than an hour each time.

The latest installment of the *Call of Duty* games achieved an
even greater milestone. *Call of Duty: Black Ops II,* released in
November 2012, took just *sixteen days* to gross $1 billion. To date,
the *Call of Duty* franchise has "exceeded worldwide ticket sales
produced by even Hollywood's heaviest hitters, the *Star Wars* and
Harry Potter series of films."

King then shifts his focus to movies in an attempt to show that
Americans don't really care that much for violence:

> [I]f you look at the dozen top-grossing films of 2012, you
> see an interesting thing: only one (*Skyfall*) features gun vio-
> lence. Three of the most popular were animated cartoons, one
> is an R-rated comedy, and three (*The Avengers, The Dark Knight
> Rises,* and *The Amazing Spider-Man*) are superhero films. . . .
> Superhero movies and comic books teach a lesson that runs di-
> rectly counter to the culture-of-violence idea: guns are for bad
> guys too cowardly to fight like men.

It's honestly as though he were living in a different world. This
entire statement is completely false. Has he even seen these movies? *The Avengers* and *Dark Knight Rises* both feature plenty of gun
violence—and not just by the "bad guys," as he claims. In addition,
why is he stopping at the top twelve? Maybe because if you look at
the top twenty instead, you find *Django Unchained* and *Taken 2,*
movies that both feature an incredible amount of gun violence? In
Taken 2 the protagonist acts as though his gun is virtually melded
to his hand.

A Real Dark Knight

The man accused of killing twelve people in Aurora, Colorado, during a screening of *The Dark Knight Rises* told authorities that he "was The Joker"—the principal villain in the previous Batman movie, *The Dark Knight*. The killer even dyed his hair to match the Joker's.

And why does King choose to include only movies with gunplay? Watching violent media can be damaging to children regardless of whether a character uses a gun, or, in the case of *The Hunger Games* (the third-highest-grossing film in the United States in 2012) kids kill other kids in all kinds of increasingly violent ways. *The Hunger Games,* by the way, was a young adult book and the movie version was marketed directly to teens.

When it comes to television, King admits that there's plenty of violence, but then, using every ounce of creativity he can muster, he comes up with another convenient excuse: "There are violent programs on television. . . . But the only one that seems to appeal to teens is AMC's *The Walking Dead*. There's plenty of gunplay in that one, but almost all of it is directed at people who have already expired."

So the fact that this show has zombies, not humans, being shot at and hit over the head with baseball bats makes it okay for kids to watch? Got it—thanks for clearing that up.

The more King goes through a list of specific titles and genres and tries to excuse them, the more obvious it is that we have the stronger argument. When you have truth on your side you don't need to do things like explain why killing zombies is really okay or why movies based on comic books shouldn't count.

* * *

At the end of the book I have some ideas about what we can do, as parents and as a community, to stop the dangerous trajectory we're on and help the healing begin. It's about taking personal responsibility for ourselves and our families and applying some old-fashioned common sense. While I have no illusions that it will be as easy as it sounds, I also have no doubt about where we're headed if we don't try.

However, we all know that there are two sides to this debate about violence in America: the killer and the weapon. I choose to focus on the former because I firmly believe that people make choices; the weapon is only an instrument used to carry out those choices. We don't, for example, blame the electric chair for putting an inmate to death; we blame the inmate's decisions earlier in life that brought him to that place.

A lot of people disagree. They find it easier to blame the weapon—especially when that weapon is a gun. If a boy stabs a cat to death with a steak knife, society doesn't debate the knife, it debates how the boy got that way. We look at his life, his upbringing, his schooling, his friends, his medications, and what he does in his spare time. But if that same boy uses a gun to kill that cat, everything changes. All of a sudden it's not about the boy, it's about the weapon. What kind of gun was it? How many rounds did it hold? How did he get it? Why didn't it have a trigger guard? While there are certainly legitimate questions to be asked in the wake of a violent act, gun crimes seem to divert attention from where it should really be: on the person committing the act.

One of the most popular arguments made in support of gun control is the idea that other countries have strict gun control laws and very few gun crimes. We looked at why that argument is wrong in Part One, when we saw how Switzerland has lots of firearms but very few gun-related crimes. Semi-automatics can be legally purchased there and, according to *Time*, "nobody bats an eye at the sight of a civilian riding a bus, bike or motorcycle to the shooting range, with a rifle slung across the shoulder."

Yet, despite all of that, Switzerland experiences about 0.5 gun homicides per 100,000 people annually. The rate in the United States is about six times higher.

The difference between the United States and Switzerland is not the guns; it's the people and the culture. "Social conditions are fundamental in deterring crime," Peter Squires, professor of criminology and public policy at the University of Brighton in Great Britain, told *Time*. Squires has "studied gun violence in different countries and concluded that a 'culture of support,' rather than focus on individualism, can deter mass killings."

Unfortunately, that argument, even from a guy in Great Britain, is not going to persuade those who believe that the only thing that can deter mass killings is a ban on the weapons sometimes used to commit them.

So, for now, I'll be happy to end with some apparent common ground that President Barack Obama and I share on this issue. During a recent trip to Chicago, a city riddled with gun violence despite very strict control measures, Obama acknowledged that perhaps guns shouldn't really be blamed for everything. "[T]his is not just a gun issue," he said. "It's also an issue of the kinds of communities that we're building."

And, I believe, the kinds of kids we're raising.

THE WAY FORWARD

There are plenty of radical things we can do—and many of them have already been proposed—that will make no real difference. For some people, that's okay. They would rather achieve a political goal or "do something" bold so they can sleep better at night, even if that means the underlying problem never gets solved.

I'm not one of those people. And I don't think you are, either.

That doesn't mean we have to sit on our hands. Far from it. But a reactionary response to a terrible event is how we ended up with Japanese internment camps. And a heavy-handed government-knows-best response is how we ended up with Prohibition—which, by the way, is still the only constitutional amendment to ever have been repealed.

Come to think of it, there is a lot in common between the way controllists now talk about guns and the way they talked about alcohol before Prohibition. Invoking terms like "public health crisis" and "a moral issue" has been done before, and, of course both alcohol and guns have been targeted as the root cause of whatever is wrong with society.

If we just took the alcohol away, everything would be solved.

That's not hyperbole; it's literally the way some people felt about alcohol back then. In a sermon celebrating Prohibition in January 1920, the Reverend Billy Sunday proclaimed:

The reign of tears is over. The slums will soon be a memory. We will turn our prisons into factories and our jails into storehouses and corncribs. Men will walk upright now, women will smile, and the children will laugh. Hell will be forever for rent.

Not quite. What actually happened was that liquor went underground. Speakeasy clubs formed (according to the National Archives, 30,000–100,000 such clubs opened in the first five years in New York City alone), mob bosses and organized crime rose to power, and everyone else just got a lot more creative. According to the archives, "People found clever ways to evade Prohibition agents. They carried hip flasks, hollowed canes, false books, and the like."

Prohibition may have made some people feel good, but it did nothing to solve the underlying problem. Gun control works the same way. There are, however, a couple of big differences between the prohibitionists of the twentieth century and the controllists of today. First, the people behind these efforts have changed. Progressives and Do-Gooders brought us alcohol prohibition, but gun prohibition is being championed by Progressives, Do-Gooders, *and* the Marxists. This a far more lethal combination.

The other major difference is that the right to alcohol was not enshrined by our Framers in the Constitution. So while the tactics used to change public perception may be similar, the stakes are not. If prohibiting alcohol was a test of the government's potential to be a nanny, prohibiting guns is a test of its potential to be a tyrant.

Those who are serious about finding real solutions to gun violence understand that effective change has to come from the bottom up. That means harnessing the collective grief we all feel after a tragedy and using it to promote real change—not in statutory codes, but in the hearts and minds of people, especially our children. We must be honest enough about our failings to be willing to take another look at our schools—how we educate our kids and how we protect them while we're doing it; to rethink personal responsibility—as parents and as law-abiding gun owners; and to engage in reasonable debate with reasonable people who are willing to have honest conversations—not as gun-grabbing ideologues, but as parents and friends.

With those principles as our foundation, let's take a look at how we can improve on both sides of the issue.

Guns

For all the reasons explained in Part One, I am not in favor of more gun control (sorry, "gun safety") legislation. I do not believe that government can heal the broken hearts and minds of those who think that picking up a weapon is the answer. However, there are still plenty of commonsense things we can do.

First, while it's virtually impossible to know exactly how many existing gun control laws are on the books, no one disputes that it's a staggeringly high number. However, many of those laws are either not enforced to their fullest extent or are disregarded altogether. Call me crazy, but I'd rather hold off on rushing a bunch of new laws through in the wake of tragedy until we can reasonably assess whether the ones we already have actually work.

Here's one example: When purchasing a gun from a licensed dealer, a buyer must fill out ATF form 4473 for a background check. Lying on this form is a felony punishable by up to ten years in prison. According to a report done for the Department of Justice, 72,600 people lied on this form in 2010 alone. Of those, "prosecutors pursued *just 44*." Not 44 percent: 44 total cases. In other words, only .06 percent of all people who committed this *felony* by lying on an ATF form were prosecuted. Does something about that seem wrong to you?

Given how badly most gun control advocates want to expand the background check system, it might be nice if we first pushed to fix the system we have. After all, if we don't prosecute those who lie on this form, then what is the point of the form? People with a clear issue in their past will just lie and hope for the best, while everyone else still has to go through the motions.

When the NRA brought these lack of prosecutions up to Joe Biden, they reported that he responded by saying, "[W]e simply don't have the time or manpower to prosecute everybody who lies on a form, that checks a wrong box, that answers a question inaccurately."

You don't have the time? To enforce the law? To prosecute felons?

It's incredible that a federal government that won't use the power we've already given it is now asking for so much more. But even if we prosecuted everyone who lies on their forms, the background check system itself would still be broken. The National Instant Criminal Background Check System (NICS) depends on certain federal agencies, like the Defense Department, along with each individual state, to continually supply the system with lists of those who have a criminal record, have failed drug tests, or have been judged mentally ill.

But those updates just aren't happening. The Defense Department has yet to report much of anything and, according to Newark, New Jersey, mayor Cory Booker—who agrees that the system is flawed—"19 states have provided fewer than 100 records of individuals disqualified on mental health grounds" since the NICS began. And, surprise, surprise, Congress hasn't been helping. From 2009 to 2011 they "appropriated just 5.3 percent of the total authorized amount," leaving the NICS underfunded. Just to be clear: I'm not fan of this system, but don't tell me how great it would be to expand background checks when we clearly can't even manage what we already have. And while several of President Obama's recent executive orders on gun control were focused on some of these problems, we're a long way off from fixing them.

The next thing we can do is make it easier to put gun traffickers away. Since I've included so many of Mayor Bloomberg's quotes that I disagree with in this book, here's one that I am with him on:

> [M]ake gun trafficking a federal crime. Every year, illegal trafficking channels put tens of thousands of guns in the hands of criminals. But there is no clear and effective statute that makes gun trafficking a federal crime. Prosecutors who want to combat traffickers have no choice but to rely on a weak law that prohibits "engaging in the business of selling guns without a federal license," which carries the *same punishment as trafficking chicken or livestock*. (emphasis added)

If we all agree that keeping guns away from criminals is the goal, then this is just absurd. A Department of Justice study from 2001 revealed that almost 79 percent of criminals got their gun somewhere other than a retail store. And that makes sense—people who acquire things with the intent of using them for harm generally don't walk into a Walmart to buy them.

Finally, I do believe that putting armed and trained officers in our schools will help save lives. In Simpsonville, South Carolina, a town of about eighteen thousand, an officer who previously worked in a community service office relocated his desk to the elementary school. "All I needed from the school is a desk and Wi-Fi," the officer said. "[I]t didn't cost a dime."

So far, the teachers love it, the kids love the officer and give him high fives every day, and the parents feel safer. As he told NBC News, in explaining why he made the move, "I'd rather be here and not be needed, than be needed and not be here."

This is a model that can and should be replicated across the country—and, in many cases, it won't require any hard decisions about spending or budgets, just a strong majority of people who want to do something that will actually make a difference.

Entertainment Violence

By now you've seen that entertainment violence is not the red herring that those from the industry, along with the controllists who think that banning guns is the only answer to all of society's ills, say it is. The evidence of its impact on our children is, for anyone willing to give it a fair hearing, indisputable.

What's also indisputable is how hard it is to shield our kids from these images. As a father of four, I've experienced this first-hand. We try so hard as parents to be role models and to show our kids the right path, but eventually we have to let go. When that time comes—and it always will—all we can do is pray that they remember what we've tried to teach them. It's not foolproof, but if we do our jobs, they'll usually do theirs.

In the meantime, there is plenty we can do. First, know the ratings system. All video games sold in stores are assigned a rating by the Entertainment Software Ratings Board (ESRB). While there are plenty of problems with these ratings (for example, they are determined based on clips provided by the manufacturers, not after someone has actually played the game), it's still important for parents to understand how they work.

The highest rating a game can earn is AO, for "Adults Only."

These games "[m]ay include prolonged scenes of intense violence, graphic sexual content and/or gambling with real currency."

Games that obtain an AO rating solely due to violence are extraordinarily rare. Sexual or pornographic behavior will do it; gambling will make the cut—but no amount of violence appears to be sufficient for the ESRB to slap a game as AO. The only notable exception to this rule was the gruesome game *Manhunt 2*, which was first given an AO rating, later revised to M after the manufacturer blurred some of the worst scenes. (Ironically, the Wii version of the game, in which you physically use the controller to beat, hack, bludgeon, strangle, and stab people to death, also has an M rating.)

Part of the reason why games generally don't receive an AO rating is that it's essentially equivalent to a movie that gets a NC-17 rating: no one can make any money from it. All of the major gaming platforms prohibit AO-rated games from being licensed on their consoles, and major retailers won't sell them. As a result, publishers will almost always modify and resubmit their games to get their rating improved, or they'll cancel the title altogether.

For parents, the key takeaway is that if your child is playing an AO-rated game, they're probably playing it on a PC—and it's probably full of content that would appall you. But, the reality is that AO games are not that common, which is why the next ratings level down is really where the bulk of the violence occurs. That level, called M for "Mature," implies that a game contains "content [that] is generally suitable for ages 17 and up. May contain intense violence, blood and gore, sexual content and/or strong language." In both M- and AO-rated games the violence is labeled as "intense," the only difference being that AO ratings mean "prolonged sequences" of violence.

Since this point is so often misunderstood, I'm going to repeat it again: M-rated games are *the top rating a commercially available game can have.* Do not be fooled into thinking that because a game is rated M instead AO that it's fine—it may very well not be. Only you can judge what's appropriate for your child. You wouldn't let some group of unknown people decide what your kids eat every day—why let them decide what's okay for them to watch?

Moving to the next category, T for Teen has "content [that] is generally suitable for ages 13 and up. May contain violence, suggestive themes, crude humor, minimal blood, simulated gambling and/or infrequent use of strong language." Many people hear this rating and immediately equate it to PG-13, "parental guidance suggested," but Colonel Grossman says that's a mistake: T-rated games, he believes, are never for kids under thirteen, even *with* parental guidance.

Lastly, there is E, for "Everyone." These games can contain "minimal cartoon, fantasy or mild violence and/or infrequent use of mild language." But be careful as there is also an E for an "Everyone 10+" rating—so make sure to check which one you are actually getting.

Understanding these ratings is important—but it would not be a terrible idea to play the games yourself so that you can really see what your kids will be spending their time with. Make it something fun with your kids—they can play a game (maybe rent a title they are interested in for a night before you commit to purchasing it) only if you can play it, too. You can even bet a household chore on who wins—just make sure you don't mind taking out the trash and emptying the dishwasher, because you're not going to come out on top very often.

But while educating parents about these games is a start, we can do more. Our children often spend far too much time immersed in electronic media. Personal interactions suffer as a result. A phone call is replaced by a text; a night out is replaced by Facebook or by remotely playing the same online game together.

And this will only continue to get worse. As our technology advances and virtual reality becomes more and more realistic, our children may no longer feel a need to spend time with actual people. This is coming faster than you think. Technologists have shown me what's to come and it is as awe-inspiring as it is frightening. If we have not done the hard work of reconnecting with our families and of properly conditioning our kids before this arrives, it will already be too late.

With that in mind, why not try to "detox" for a week? Turn off the television, the video games, and the iPads and spend real time together as a family. Yes, there will be complaining, and no, it won't be easy—but things that have life-changing potential rarely are. I can promise you this from someone who has tried it: you will truly be amazed at the difference unplugging can make. When my family and I visit our ranch home, which has no electricity or cellular service, the world becomes our playground. My eight-year-old spent most of his time chasing after the cows to keep them away from the horses' hay and my six-year-old learned how to shoot her BB gun and put puzzles together. They now look forward to our days at the ranch more than any other vacation.

And why stop at home? What if we could pass this detox on to everyone in your children's school? In 2004, the Stanford University Medical School and the Stanford Prevention Research Center developed the "Student Media Awareness to Reduce Television" (SMART) curriculum for third- and fourth-grade students. This program was systematically designed to educate students and ultimately convince kids to turn off the TV, movies, and video games. The curriculum culminates in a ten-day TV turnoff "challenge." After this "detox" the impact is so positive, and children feel so good (both about themselves and in the sense of physical well-being), that most are then willing to put themselves on a longer-term TV "budget" or "diet."

Immediately after the release of the Stanford SMART curriculum, Kristine Paulsen at Delta-Schoolcraft (Michigan) Intermediate School District began developing the "Take the Challenge—Take Charge" program (www.TakeTheChallengeNow .net). This program expanded the SMART concept into a preschool through twelfth grade curriculum so that almost all families can use it. The website has lesson plans, ideas for family activities, and links to more great research on the topic.

I truly believe that getting serious about our current laws, taking personal responsibility for our families, and thinking out of the box about ways we can further protect our kids will do more to change our course than a thousand new rules and regulations. We know from experience that our government very often creates many of the problems we face, and they almost always make these problems worse while they are "trying to solve" them. That's why I know that the way forward cannot be found in the halls of Congress, it can only be found in the rooms of our homes and the streets of our neighborhoods.

I'd like to think that President Obama agrees. He recently explained why so many of the school massacres we've come to know by heart could not have been prevented by any law.

"When a child opens fire on another child," he said, "there's a hole in that child's heart that government can't fill. Only community and parents and teachers and clergy can fill that hole."

Mr. President—this is one thing that you are absolutely right about. So let's come together and fill those hearts with hope, brains with knowledge, and souls with faith. Once we do, a gun will stop symbolizing violence and fear and go back to symbolizing what it always has: security and freedom.

NOTES

AUTHOR'S NOTE

PAGE XI: " 'We can do better. We must do something.' " Richard Blumenthal, "Mourning a Lost Son; Guns in America; Arming the Teachers," *Piers Morgan Tonight*, CNN, December 20, 2012, http://bit.ly/11hfP4L. • " 'We must act, we must act, we must act.' " Eliza Collins, "Thousands Rally in Washington for Gun Control," *USA Today*, January 26, 2013, http://usat.ly/11hfQ8O. • **PAGE XII:** "fewer people had been struck by trains that year," Ted Mann, "Track Deaths Rare," *Wall Street Journal*, January 28, 2013, http://on.wsj.com/11hfVJN. • **PAGE XIII:** " 'shouldn't we also quit marketing murder as a game?' " David Axelrod, "In NFL post-game: an ad for shoot 'em up video game. All for curbing weapons of war. But shouldn't we also quit marketing murder as a game?" December 17, 2012, 12:57AM, Twitter post, https://twitter.com/davidaxelrod/status/280552289360560128.

PART ONE: THE TRUTH ABOUT GUNS

PAGE 1: "depicting intense gun violence in movies" "Hollywood A-Listers Called Hypocrites on Issue of Gun Violence in 'Demand a Plan' Response Video," *foxnews.com*, January 2, 2013, http://fxn.ws/11hfM8W.

IT'S TIME FOR AMERICA TO HAVE A CONVERSATION ABOUT GUNS.

PAGE 2: " 'before all those kids in Connecticut died today' " Rep. Carolyn McCarthy, *Rachel Maddow Show*, MSNBC, December 14, 2012, http://on.today.com/11hdtmk. • " 'we're going to have a national conversation on the subject' " Cindy Handler, "How to Talk About Gun Violence," *The Blog* blog at *huffingtonpost.com*, January 11, 2013, http://huff.to/WF4bk4.

WE SHOULD START DRAFTING A BILL TO ENSURE NEWTOWN NEVER HAPPENS AGAIN.

PAGE 2: " 'It'll be ready on the first day' " Sen. Diane Feinstein, interview by David Gregory, *Meet the Press*, NBC, December 16, 2012, http://nbcnews.to/161qJ1i.

GUNS ARE LETHAL.

PAGE 3: " 'not with knives, but with automatic weapons' " Nicholas Kristof, interview by Piers Morgan, *Piers Morgan Tonight*, CNN, January 8, 2013, http://bit.ly/11heICb. • "When [a .223-caliber round] hits a human body, the effects are devastating" Gen. Stanley McChrystal, "Gen. McChrystal: Assault Rifles Are for Battlefields, Not Schools," *Morning Joe*, MSNBC, January 8, 2013, http://on.msnbc.com/11hfE9t. • **PAGE 4:** "as fertilizer (ammonium nitrate), a common cleaning solvent (liquid

nitromethane), and diesel fuel" Jo Thomas, "For First Time, Woman Says McVeigh Told of Bomb Plan," *New York Times*, April 30, 1997, http://nyti.ms/11hfjns, See also: Jon Ronson, "Conspirators," *Guardian,* May 4, 2001. • **"was carried out with a bomb"** Pete Winn, "The Worst School Massacre in American History Was 'Gun Free,' " *cnsnews.com*, September 12, 2012, http://bit.ly/11hfizM.

NO ONE WANTS TO TAKE YOUR GUNS AWAY

PAGE 4: " 'No one is saying that people's guns should be taken away' " Don Lemon, "Aurora and the Politics of Guns," *CNN Newsroom*, CNN, July 22, 2012, http://bit.ly/101bCkj. • " **'Nobody questions the Second Amendment's right to bear arms'** " "Dannel Malloy, Michael Bloomberg, Dianne Feinstein, Bill Bennett, David Brooks, Randi Weingarten, Tom Ridge, Michael Eric Dyson, Pete Williams," *Meet the Press*, NBC, December 16, 2012, http://nbcnews.to/11hffE0. • " **'I want to get rid of these killing machine assault weapons off the street'** " Piers Morgan, "Guns in America," *Piers Morgan Tonight*, CNN, January 7, 2013, http://bit.ly/10jLcfY. • **PAGE 5:** " **'No serious person, including Obama, is even proposing taking away owned guns'** " Touré, " 'Gun grabber' is a mythical boogeyman. No serious person, including Obama, is even proposing taking away owned guns. #StopFear mongering," February 16, 2013, 6:22AM, Twitter post, https://twitter.com/Toure/status/302784941337501696. • **PAGE 6:** **"74 percent of Americans oppose a ban on the possession of handguns"** "Guns," *gallup.com*, accessed March 5, 2013, http://bit.ly/LLI5U0. • " **'an outright ban, picking up every one of them'** " Warner Todd Huston, " 'Turn 'em All In' Feinstein Said She Wanted All Guns Banned," *breitbart.com*, January 1, 2013, http://bit.ly/11hfajU. • **PAGE 7:** " **'What we need to do is change the way in which people think about guns'** " "Eric Holder: Gun Owners Should 'Cower' in Shame Like Smokers," *newsbusters.org*, January 10, 2013, http://bit.ly/11hf6AF. • **"really brainwash people into thinking about guns in a vastly different way"** "Eric Holder: Gun Owners Should 'Cower' in Shame Like Smokers," *news busters.org*, January 10, 2013, http://bit.ly/11hf6AF. • " **'not hunt elementary school children'** " Katherine Fung, "Don Lemon: 'We Need to Get Guns and Bullets and Automatic Weapons Off the Streets' (Video)," *huffingtonpost.com*, December 17, 2012, http://huff.to/11heSJA. • **PAGE 8:** " **'We don't need guns. We have 10,000 murders a year'** " "America's Assault Weapons; Attorneys for Alleged Rape Victim in Ohio and Her Alleged Rapist Argue Their Sides as Case Stirs Controversy Across Social Media," *Piers Morgan Tonight*, CNN, January 8, 2013, http://bit.ly/11heICb. • " **'the United States should ban private gun ownership entirely, or almost entirely'** " Jeff McMahan, "Why Gun 'Control' Is Not Enough," *Opinionator* blog at *nytimes.com*, December 19, 2012, http://nyti.ms/11heQS7. • " **'aggressive efforts to reduce the supply of existing weapons, no one can be safer'** " "Taming the Monster: Get Rid of the Guns: More Firearms Won't Make America Safer—They Will Only Accelerate and Intensify the Heartache and Bloodshed," *Los Angeles Times*, December 28, 1993, http://lat.ms/11hf4bK. • **PAGE 9:** **"banning all guns—is not going to happen."** Lexington, "The Gun Control that Works: No Guns," *The Economist*, 15 December 2012, http://econ.st/11heY42. • " **'I totally respect and admire the Constitution and the Second Amendment'** " Piers Morgan, "California School Shooting; America and Assault Rifles," *Piers Morgan Tonight*, CNN, January 10, 2013, http://bit.ly/11heHOG. • " **'in an ideal world, I'd have all guns gone'** " Piers Morgan, "California School Shooting; America and Assault Rifles," *Piers Morgan Tonight*, CNN, January 10, 2013, http://bit.ly/11heHOG. • **PAGE 10:** **"Morgan had this exchange on his show"** "America's Assault Weapons; Attorneys for Alleged Rape Victim in Ohio and Her Alleged Rapist Argue Their Sides as Case Stirs Controversy Across Social Media," *Piers Morgan Tonight*, CNN, January 8, 2013, http://bit.ly/11heICb. • **Here's a brief summary of how their gun ban came to be"** "Britain's Changing Firearms Laws," *BBC*

News, 12 November 2007, http://news.bbc.co.uk/2/hi/uk_news/7056245.stm. • **"This expired after two years"** Clayton Cramer, "Gun Control: Political Fears Trump Crime Control," *Maine Law Review 61*, no.1 (2009): 58–81, http://bit.ly/16Jjlc5. • **PAGE 11: " 'the ownership of firearms ceased to be a right of Englishmen, and instead became a privilege' "** Clayton Cramer, "Gun Control: Political Fears Trump Crime Control," *Maine Law Review 61*, no.1 (2009): 58–81, http://bit.ly/16Jjlc5. • **"An update to the Firearms Act is passed that raises the minimum age to buy a gun, gives police more power to regulate licenses"** "Firearms Act, 1937," Page 1, http://dvc.org.uk/dunblane/fa1937.pdf • **"The home secretary also rules that self-defense is no longer a valid reason to be granted a gun certificate"** Malcolm, Joyce Lee, *Guns and Violence: The English Experience*, 2002, Page 160, http://bit.ly/16JeuaU. • **"show good reason for carrying ammunition and guns"** "Prohibited Weapons Defined by section 5 Firearms Act 1968 as Amended," *The Crown Prosecution Service: Legal Resources*, http://www.cps.gov.uk/legal/d_to_g/firearms/#a14.

WELL, CAN'T WE AT LEAST CLARIFY THE SECOND AMENDMENT?

PAGE 12: "Is there an argument for the Second Amendment to be repealed and to be clarified and be redrafted" Piers Morgan, "Remembering Olivia Engel; Gun Control in America; Interview with Carolyn McCarthy, Ron Barber," *Piers Morgan Tonight*, CNN, December 18, 2012, http://bit.ly/11hag6q.

THAT MAY BE, BUT EVEN THOMAS JEFFERSON WANTED THE SECOND AMENDMENT TO EXPIRE.

PAGE 13: " 'said that it should be revisited every 20 years to see if it is still appropriate' " Christopher Kennedy Lawford, "Guns in America," *Piers Morgan Tonight*, CNN, January 7, 2013, http://bit.ly/10jLcfY. • **PAGE 14: "a man who is a self-described 'author, activist and actor' "** Christopher Kennedy Lawford, "Home," *christopherkennedylawford.com*, accessed March 3, 2013, http://christopherkennedylawford.com. • **" 'it is an act of force and not of right' "** Thomas Jefferson, letter to James Madison, September 6, 1789, http://bit.ly/11heACz.

THE UNITED STATES HAS THE HIGHEST GUN MURDER RATE IN THE DEVELOPED WORLD.

PAGE 16: " 'murder and gun crime of any of the civilized countries of this world' " Piers Morgan, "Remembering Olivia Engel; Gun Control in America; Interview with Carolyn McCarthy, Ron Barber," *Piers Morgan Tonight*, CNN, December 18, 2012, http://bit.ly/11hag6p. • **"the U.S. murder rate was 4.7 per 100,000"** William J. Krouse, Gun Control Legislation, report prepared for Members and Committees of Congress, 12 Cong., 2d sess., 2012, Committee Print, 10, http://bit.ly/wvkslu. • **"the gun murder rate was 3.2"** William J. Krouse, Gun Control Legislation, report prepared for Members and Committees of Congress, 12 Cong., 2d sess., 2012, Committee Print, 10,http://bit.ly/wvkslu. • **"homicide rates in Russia and Brazil have averaged about four to five times higher than ours"** "Intentional Homicide, Count and Rate per 100,000 Population (1995–2011)," 2011 Global Study on Homicide: Trends/Contexts/Data (Vienna: United Nations Office on Drugs and Crime , 2011), http://bit.ly/16JjRqx. • **"the United States is somewhere near the mid-range"** Olga Khazan, "Here's How U.S. Gun Violence Compares with the Rest of the World," *Washington Post*, December 14, 2012, http://wapo.st/16JjY5t. • **"higher rates of gun ownership correlate with fewer deaths"** Simon Rogers, "Gun Homicides and Gun Ownership Listed by Country," *Datablog* blog at *guardian.co.uk*, July 22, 2012, http://bit.ly/16Jk64R.

OKAY, BUT THE OVERALL U.S. MURDER RATE IS MUCH HIGHER THAN OTHER WEALTHY COUNTRIES.

PAGE 18: " 'tougher laws controlling private ownership of guns' " "In Other Countries, Laws Are Strict and Work," *New York Times*, December 17, 2012, http://nyti.ms/16JkfW9. • "**The U.S. homicide rate in 2011 was 4.7**" William J. Krouse, *Gun Control Legislation*, report prepared for Members and Committees of Congress, 12 Cong., 2d sess., 2012, Committee Print, 10,http://bit.ly/wvkslu. • "**the United Nations data on homicide rates for the 20 "wealthiest" countries**" Simon Rogers, "Gun Homicides and Gun Ownership Listed by Country," *Datablog* at *guardian.co.uk*, July 22, 2012, http://bit.ly/16Jk64R. • "**have rates between 0.7 and 2.5**" Simon Rogers, "Gun Homicides and Gun Ownership Listed by Country," *Datablog* at *guardian.co.uk*, July 22, 2012, http://bit.ly/16Jk64R.

BUT OTHER COUNTRIES HAVE STRICT GUN CONTROL AND VERY FEW MURDERS.

PAGE 18: " '**They have two or three murders a year. You have 11,000 to 12,000'** " Piers Morgan, "Gun Control in America; Aurora Families Speak Out," *Piers Morgan Tonight*, CNN, December 17, 2012, http://bit.ly/YZGT8r. • PAGE 19: "**reported just two gun murders and five armed robberies**" Joyce Lee Malcolm, Guns and Violence: The English Experience (Cambridge, MA: Harvard University Press, 2002) 209–16. • " '**self-defense was never a good reason for a permit**' " Joyce Lee Malcolm, "Joyce Lee Malcolm: Two Cautionary Tales of Gun Control," *Wall Street Journal*, December 26, 2012, http://on.wsj.com/16Jf20rl. • PAGE 20: "**Semi-automatic rifles were banned and shotguns were regulated like handguns**" Joyce Lee Malcolm, "Joyce Lee Malcolm: Two Cautionary Tales of Gun Control," *Wall Street Journal*, December 26, 2012, http://on.wsj.com/16Jf20r. • "**forcing lawful owners to turn them in or face ten years in prison**" Joyce Lee Malcolm, "Joyce Lee Malcolm: Two Cautionary Tales of Gun Control," *Wall Street Journal*, December 26, 2012, http://on.wsj.com/16Jf20r. • " '**killing 12 people and injuring 11 more before killing himself** " Joyce Lee Malcolm, "Joyce Lee Malcolm: Two Cautionary Tales of Gun Control," *Wall Street Journal*, December 26, 2012, http://on.wsj.com/16Jf20r. • "**from 1.1 homicides per 100,000 people in 1996 to 1.8 in 2003**" Kevin Smith ed. Sarah Osborne, Ivy Lau, and Andrew Britton, "Homicides Firearm Offences and Intimate Violence 2010/11: Supplementary Volume 2 to Crime in England and Wales 2010/11," *Home Office Statistical Bulletin*, January 2012, http://bit.ly/16Jkss9. • "**the police force was expanded by 16 percent between 2001 and 2005**" Simon Bullock and Natalie Gunning, "Police Service Strength," Home Office Statistical Bulletin, July 26, 2007, http://bit.ly/16Jf88n, See also: Amardeep Dhani, "Police Service Strength," *Home Office Statistical Bulletin*, July 26, 2012, http://bit.ly/16Jfgoh. • "**crime generally remained higher than before the Firearms Act**" Cal Flyn, "Graphic: How the Murder Rate Has Fallen," *Telegraph*, July 19, 2012, http://bit.ly/16JfqMn. • PAGE 22: "**after the laws were passed many of these same people continued to own guns**" "Australian Guns," *snopes.com*, accessed March 6, 2013, http://www.snopes.com/crime/statistics/ausguns.asp. • "**the country averaged only about 550 gun-related deaths per year**" Jenny Mouzos and Catherine Rushforth, "Firearm Related Deaths in Australia, 1991–2001," Australian Institute of Criminology, *Trends and Issues in Crime and Criminal Justice*, no. 269 (November 2003), 261–80, http://bit.ly/16JfyM0. • "**More than 650,000 guns were turned in or confiscated from 1996 to 1997 as a result of this buy-back**" Daniel Burdon, "US Would Benefit from a Gun Buyback: Labor MP," *Sunshine Coast Daily*, December 17, 2012, http://bit.ly/100vC6G. • "**bought more single-shot guns, bringing the total back to 3.2 million after about fourteen years**" Nick Ralston, "Australia Reloads as Gun Amnesties Fail to Cut Arms," *Sydney Morning Herald*, January 14, 2013, http://bit.ly/16Jkxwe. • "**averaged 82 per year from 1991 to 1996, and 58 per year from**

1997 to 2001" Jenny Mouzos and Catherine Rushforth, "Firearm Related Deaths in Australia, 1991–2001," Australian Institute of Criminology, *Trends and Issues in Crime and Criminal Justice*, no. 269 (November 2003), 261–80, http://bit.ly/16JfyM0. • **PAGE 23: "increased to about 255 per year from 1997 to 2001**" Jeanine Baker and Samara McPhedran, "Gun Laws and Sudden Death," *British Journal of Criminology* 47, no. 3 (October 2006), 455–69, http://bit.ly/11heta1. • **"those who would've used a gun instead use something else, like a knife"** Australian Institute of Criminology, "Homicide Weapon Statistics," accessed March 6, 2013, http://bit.ly/TDJ7WU. • **" 'NFA [the 1996–97 National Firearms Agreement] did not have any large effects on reducing firearm homicide or suicide rates' "** Wang-Sheng Lee and Sandy Suardi, "The Australian Firearms Buyback and Its Effect on Gun Deaths," *Melbourne Institute Working Paper Series*, Working Paper, no. 17/08 (August 2008), http://bit .ly/100vFQ5. • **PAGE 24: " 'gun buy-back and restrictive legislative changes had no influence on firearm homicide' "** Jeanine Baker and Samara McPhedran, "Gun Laws and Sudden Death," *British Journal of Criminology* 47, no. 3 (October 2006), 455–469, http://bit.ly/11heta1. • **"from about 6,000 in 1996 to around 10,000 between 1998 and 2001"** Australian Institute of Criminology, "Australian Crime: Robbery Statistics," accessed March 18, 2013, http://bit.ly/ZM6K2O. • **"Japan has imposed strict gun control for centuries"** David Kopel, "Japanese Gun Control," Asia Pacific Law Review 2 (1993), 26–52, http://bit.ly/YpMghY. • **"but handguns are banned"** Eric Talmadge, "Around World, Gun Rules, and Results, Vary Wildly," *USA Today*, January 27, 2013, http://usat.ly/11helHJ. • **"Switzerland had a gun homicide rate of 0.5 per 100,000 people in 2010"** Helena Bachmann, "The Swiss Difference: A Gun Culture That Works," *Time*, December 20, 2012, http://ti.me/11h4LEN. • **"Their overall homicide rate was 0.7"** "Intentional Homicide, Count and Rate per 100,000 Population (1995–2011)," 2011 Global Study on Homicide: Trends/ Contexts/Data (Vienna: United Nations Office on Drugs and Crime, 2011), http:// bit.ly/16JkTTx. • **"well below other gun-control havens like Australia (1.0), the UK (1.2) and Canada (1.6)"** "Intentional Homicide, Count and Rate per 100,000 Population (1995–2011)," 2011 Global Study on Homicide: Trends/Contexts/Data (Vienna: United Nations Office on Drugs and Crime, 2011), http://bit.ly/16JkTTx. • **PAGE 25: "the lowest rates of gun ownership in Europe at 3.9 per capita"** Aaron Karp, "Completing the Count: Civilian Firearms," Small Arms Survey 2007: Guns and the City (2007), http://bit.ly/16Jg0tt. • **"all have lower murder rates than The Netherlands—and far more guns per capita"** "Intentional Homicide, Count and Rate per 100,000 Population (1995–2011)," 2011 Global Study on Homicide: Trends/ Contexts/Data (Vienna: United Nations Office on Drugs and Crime, 2011), http://bit .ly/16JkTTx. • **"D.C.'s handgun . . . went into effect in early 1977"** "A History of D.C. Gun Ban," *Washington Post*, June 26, 2008, http://wapo.st/16JgcJj. • **"D.C.'s murder rate ranked in top four among the fifty largest U.S. cities"** John R. Lott, Jr., More Guns, Less Crime, 3rd ed. (Chicago: University of Chicago Press, 2010), 306–307. • **"suddenly stopped falling and instead rose slightly to 23 in the five years afterward"** "D.C.'s Flawed Reasoning," *Washington Times*, September 7, 2007, http://bit .ly/16JgK1X. • **PAGE 26: "Chicago's murder rate fell from being 8.1 times greater than its neighbors in 1977 to 5.5 times in 1982, and then went way up to 12 times greater in 1987"** "D.C.'s Flawed Reasoning," *Washington Times*, September 7, 2007, http://bit.ly/16JgK1X. • **"there were 1.5 million active licenses in 1998 and only 200,000 four years later"** Associated Press, "State Gun Licenses Plung," *Cape Cod Times*, August 20, 2002, http://bit.ly/16JgSOO. • **"gunshot injuries are up, according to FBI and state data"** MacQuarrie, Brian, "Gun Crimes Increase in Massachusetts Despite Tough Gun Laws,"*Boston Globe*, February 3, 2013, http://bo.st/16JgWOK. • **" 'a striking increase from the 65 in 1998' "** Brian MacQuarrie, "Gun Crimes Increase in Massachusetts Despite Tough Gun Laws," *Boston Globe*, February 3, 2013, http://bo.st/16JgWOK. • "from aggravated assault (up 26.7 percent) to armed robbery (up 20.7 percent)—also increased" Brian MacQuarrie, "Gun Crimes Increase in Massachusetts Despite Tough Gun Laws," *Boston Globe*, February 3, 2013, http://bo.st/16JgWOK. • PAGE 27: "the state's lowest per capita homicide rate occurred in 1997" "Massachusetts Crime Rates 1960–2011," *disastercenter.com*, accessed March 6, 2013, http://bit.ly/MPCJLO. • "the homicide rate over that same time period was down 31 percent" "United States Crime Rates 1960–2011," *disastercenter.com*, accessed March 6, 2013, http://bit.ly/Vhgor.

THE UNITED STATES IS UNIQUE IN SUFFERING FROM GUN MASSACRES.

PAGE 28: " 'And we've just got to stop this' " Lynn Sweet, "Bloomberg on Only in America: We Kill People," Lynn Sweet: *The Scoop from Washington blog* at *suntimes .com*, December 16, 2012, http://bit.ly/11hedYG. • " 'the problem that America has with gun massacres' " Rachel Maddow, *Rachel Maddow Show*, MSNBC, January 11, 2011, http://nbcnews.to/11he9It. • "he murdered 69 people" "Norwegian Youth Party to Host Summer Camp, Two Years After Anders Breivik," *Telegraph*, January 30, 2013, http://bit.ly/100vMuX. • "on November 26, 2008, 164 people were killed" Harmeet Sha Singh, "India Remembers Mumbai Dead," *cnn.com*, November 26, 2010, http://bit.ly/11he5bA. • PAGE 29: "sixteen kindergartners and their teacher were killed" John Lott, "Think Tough Gun Laws Keep Europeans Safe? Think again . . . ," *foxnews.com*, June 10, 2010, http://fxn.ws/ZXBTRa. • "Two nine-month-old babies and one day-care worker were killed" Bruno Waterfield and John Bingham, "Belgium 'Joker' Creche Killer Snorted with Laughter in Police Interrogation," *Telegraph*, January 24, 2009, http://bit.ly/11hdUgF. • "He murdered eight children and seriously wounded thirteen other kids, along with two teachers" "Japan Mourns School Victims," *cnn.com*, June 10, 2001, http://bit.ly/100vUur. • "China has suppressed and censored much of the news" Edward Wong, "Fifth Deadly Attack on a School Haunts China," *New York Times*, May 12, 2010, http://nyti.ms/11hdYNo. • "Eight were reported to be killed" "China Executes Killer of Eight School Children," *BBC News*, April 28, 2010, http://bbc.in/aJDhN6. • PAGE 30: "stabbed sixteen students and a teacher in an elementary school" Jaime FlorCruz, "Execution Does Not Stop Chinese Knife Attack," *cnn.com*, May 3, 2010, http://bit.ly/100vZy2. • "stabbed twenty-eight students, two teachers, and one security guard in a kindergarten" Jaime FlorCruz, "Execution Does Not Stop Chinese Knife Attack," *cnn.com*, May 3, 2010, http://bit.ly/100vZy2. • "armed with a hammer attacked children in a pre-school" Jaime FlorCruz, "Execution Does Not Stop Chinese Knife Attack," *cnn.com*, May 3, 2010, http://bit.ly/100vZy2. • "murdered seven children and two adults and injured eleven others" Christopher Bodeen, "9 Killed in Latest Attack at China School," Associated Press, May 12, 2010, http://bit.ly/11hdKWp. • "killing three children and one teacher" "Man Held Over Fatal Knife Attack at China Kindergarten," *BBC News*, August 4, 2010, http://bbc.in/aTu1Zi. • "slashed eight children" "Eight Children Hurt in China School Attack," *BBC News*, August 29, 2011, http://bbc.in/oP5EKx. • "murdered a one-year-old and a four-year-old and four adults" Haolan Hong and Jaime FlorCruz, "6 Die in China Ax Attack," *cnn.com*, September 14, 2011, http://bit.ly/11hdSFv. • "stabbed an elderly woman and twenty-three children at an elementary school" An Baijie, "Suspect in School Knife Attack 'Feared End of the World,' " *China Daily*, December 18, 2012, http://bit.ly/161rlnB. • "with fingers and ears cut off" "22 Stabbed Students Receive Treatment in Central China," *news.xinhuanet.com*, December 15, 2012, http://bit.ly/11hdIxT. • "stabbed to death nine people and wounded four others with a knife" Associated Foreign Press, "Teen Kills Nine in Stabbing Frenzy," *Herald Sun*, August 2, 2012, http://bit.ly/100wjx1. • "Mass shootings happen with appalling regularity in Mexico, a place with restrictive gun control laws" Cave, Damien, "At a

Nation's Only Gun Shop, Looking North in Disbelief," *New York Times,* 24 July 2012. http://nyti.ms/100wlVA. • **PAGE 31: "one in February when thirteen people were killed at a party"** "Juarez Police Seek Motive in Mass Shooting," *United Press International,* February 1, 2010, http://nyti.ms/100wlVA. • **"in September, when eight were killed inside a bar"** CNN Staff Writer,"Bar Shooting in Juarez Leaves 8 Dead," *CNN,* 17 September 2010, http://bit.ly/11hD.C.9p. • **"El Paso, Texas, which was recently named the "safest large city in America"** Borunda, Daniel, "El Paso Ranked Safest Large City in U.S. for 3rd Straight Year," *El Paso Times,* February, 6, 2013, http://bit.ly/11hdDtY.

THEN WHY ARE GUN MASSACRES NOW HAPPENING MORE THAN EVER HERE IN THE UNITED STATES?

PAGE 31: " 'help them perform mass executions like today's' " Rep. Carolyn McCarthy, *Rachel Maddow Show,* MSNBC, December 14, 2012, http://on.today.com/11hdtmj. • " 'happening more frequently these days, it's because that's true' " Rachel Maddow, *Rachel Maddow Show,* MSNBC, December 17, 2012, http://nbcnews.to/11hdoiG. • **PAGE 32: "a total of 513 people have been killed in these attacks"** Mark Follman, Gavin Aronsen, and Deanna Pan, "US Mass Shootings, 1982–2012: Data from Mother Jones' Investigation," *Mother Jones,* December 28, 2012, http://bit.ly/11hdxT2. • **"3,696 people were killed in the United States by lightning"** Susan Donaldson James, "Fiancée Killed by Lightning During Surprise Wedding Proposal," *abcnews.go.com,* June 9, 2010, http://abcn.ws/11hdln3. • **PAGE 33:** " 'in direct competition with . . . a Norwegian man who killed 77' " Bob Orr and Pat Milton, "Newtown Shooter Motivated by Norway Massacre, Sources Say," *cbsnews.com,* February 18, 2013, http://cbsn.ws/100xPir. • " 'when subsequent years reveal more moderate levels' " James Alan Fox, "Mass Shootings Not Trending," *boston.com,* January 23, 2013, http://bo.st/100y0u8. • " '[M]ass shootings have not increased in number or in overall body count' " Matt Pearce, "2012 is Tragic, But Mass Shootings Not Increasing, Experts Say," *Los Angeles Times,* December 18, 2012, http://lat.ms/100xQmC. • **"there is even a slight decline in these types of killings"** John R. Lott Jr., More Guns, Less Crime, 3rd ed. (Chicago: University of Chicago Press, 2010), see also: Grant Duwe, *Mass Murder in the United States: A History* (Jefferson, NC: McFarland, 2007). • **"dropping from 43 total cases in the 1990s to 26 in the first decade of the twenty-first century"** Matt Pearce, "2012 Is Tragic, but Mass Shootings Not Increasing, Experts Say," *Los Angeles Times,* December 18, 2012, http://lat.ms/100xQmC. • **PAGE 34:** " 'even if they do not address the particular issues of mass shootings' " Greg Ridgeway, Ph.D., "Summary of Select Firearm Violence Prevention Strategies," National Rifle Association Institute for Legislative Action, January 4, 2013, http://bit.ly/11hcPWb. • **"mass killings an "epidemic"), without questioning their methodology"** Follman, Mark, and Aronsen, Gavin, and Pan Deanna, "A Guide to Mass Shootings in America," *Mother Jones,* February 27, 2013,http://bit.ly/LDEkVn. • " 'hard to defend' or 'not necessarily applied consistently' " James Alan Fox, "Mass Shootings Not Trending," *boston.com,* January 23, 2013, http://bo.st/100y0u8.

NO MASS SHOOTING HAS EVER BEEN STOPPED BY SOMEONE ELSE WITH A GUN.

PAGE 36: " 'Not a single one has ever been thwarted' " Piers Morgan, "Assault Weapons in America," *Piers Morgan Tonight,* CNN, January 9, 2013, http://bit.ly/11hD.C.js. • **"statistic of '62 mass shootings'"** Mark Follman, Gavin Aronsen, and Deanna Pan, "A Guide to Mass Shootings in America," *Mother Jones,* February 27, 2013, http://bit.ly/11hdaIe. • **PAGE 37: "hitting nine of his fellow students and killing two"** Wayne Laugesen, "A Principal and His Gun," *davekopel.org,* October 15, 1999, http://bit.ly/Vh0wsp. • **"thirty-six rounds still in his pockets,"** Bill Cole and Terri Tabor, "Armed Teachers Critics Say Putting More Weapons in Our Classrooms Will Increase Violence—No Matter Who Carries Them," *Daily Herald Arlington Heights*, March 10, 2000. • **PAGE 38: "he immediately opened fire, killing two teenage sisters"** "Nobles and Knaves," *Washington Times*, December 15, 2007. • **"armed with a rifle, two semi-automatic handguns, and a thousand rounds of ammunition, he entered the church"** Valerie Richardson, "Gunman Killed by Own Bullet, Not Volunteer's; Web Rants Targeted Christians," *Washington Times*, December 12, 2007. • " **'kill and injure as many of you [Christians] . . . as I can'** " Valerie Richardson, "Gunman Killed by Own Bullet, Not Volunteer's; Web Rants Targeted Christians," *Washington Times*, December 12, 2007. • " **'she probably saved over 100 lives'** " Patrick O'Driscoll and Oren Dorell, "Police Seek Link in Colorado Attacks," *USA Today*, October 10, 2011, http://usat.ly/11hd4Am. • **"fired several shots, wounding two students"** Kristen Hayes, "Edinboro Teen Killer Sentenced," *Pittsburgh Post-Gazette*, September 10, 1999, http://bit.ly/XqRGG8. • **"James Strand, grabbed his shotgun, followed the boy out, and persuaded him surrender"** Robert Moran and Susan Q. Stranahan, "Again Student Held in Slaying Andrew Wurst Is Accused of Killing Edinboro, PA, Teacher John Gillette and Wounding Three," *Philadelphia Inquirer*, April 6, 1998, http://bit.ly/11hd1V6. • **PAGE 39: "Terry shot him five times in the chest, killing him"** J. Neil Schulman, "Perspective on Gun Control: A Massacre We Didn't Hear About: Firearms in the Hands of Private Citizens Should Play an Important Role in Protection of the Public Safety," *Los Angeles Times*, January 1, 1992, http://lat.ms/11hcZNd. • **"a man entered the Player's Bar & Grille in Winnemucca, Nevada"** Associate Press, "Three Dead in Shooting at Winnemucca Bar," *Las Vegas Review-Journal*, May 26, 2008, http://bit.ly/gJ6pC7. • **"the man's intention was to shoot 'anyone in his line of sight . . . '** " "Gunman, Two Victims Die in Clackamas Mall Shooting," *kgw.com*, December 11, 2012, http://bit.ly/11hcUZU. • **"Meli didn't fire right away, as he was concerned about missing the gunman"** Mike Benner, "Clackamas Mall Shooter Faced Man with Concealed Weapon," *kgw.com*, December 17, 2012, http://bit.ly/100y9Ok. • **"There were estimated to be ten thousand people in the mall that day"** "Gunman, Two Victims Die in Clackamas Mall Shooting," *kgw .com*, December 11, 2012, http://bit.ly/100y9Ok.

REGARDLESS, IF WE REALLY WANT TO STOP MASS SHOOTINGS WE NEED TO BRING BACK THE ASSAULT WEAPONS BAN.

PAGE 40: " **'and drums that hold more than 10 rounds'** " Sen. Dianne Feinstein, "Feinstein to Introduce Updated Assault Weapons Bill In New Congress," *feinstein.senate .gov*, December 17, 2012, http://1.usa.gov/100yccN. • " **'from Columbine to Oak Creek'** " Sen. Dianne Feinstein, "Feinstein Introduces Bill on Assault Weapons, High-Capacity Magazines," *feinstein.senate.gov*, January 24, 2013, http://1.usa.gov/100ydxz. • **"Nothing we're going to do is going to fundamentally alter or eliminate the possibility of another mass shooting"** Hunt, Kasie,"Biden: New Gun Controls Likely Won't End Shootings," *NBC News*, 31 January 2013, http://nbcnews.to/100yh0e. • **PAGE 41: "she references a part of a 1997 study"** Sen. Dianne Feinstein, "Stopping the Spread of Deadly Assault Weapons," *feinstein.senate.gov*, accessed March 7, 2013, http://1.usa.gov/100ykt4. • " **'caused a reduction of 6.7% in gun murders'** " Jeffrey A. Roth, Christopher S. Koper, William Adams, and others, "Impact Evaluation of the Public Safety and Recreational Firearms Use Protection Act of 1994," (report, The Urban Institute, Washington, D.C., March 13, 1997), http://bit.ly/100ylx9. • " **'and local initiatives that took place simultaneously'** " Jeffrey A. Roth, Christopher S. Koper, William Adams, and others, "Impact Evaluation of the Public Safety and Recreational Firearms Use Protection Act of 1994" (report, The Urban Institute, Washington, D.C., March 13, 1997), http://bit.ly/100ylx9. • " **'we found no statistical**

evidence of post-ban decreases' " Jeffrey A. Roth, Christopher S. Koper, William Adams, and others, "Impact Evaluation of the Public Safety and Recreational Firearms Use Protection Act of 1994" (report, The Urban Institute, Washington, D.C., March 13, 1997), http://bit.ly/100ylx9. • PAGE 42: ' "[W]e cannot clearly credit the ban with any of the nation's recent drop in gun violence' " Christopher Koper with Daniel Woods and Jeffrey Roth, "An Updated Assessment of the Federal Assault Weapons Ban: Impacts on Gun Markets and Gun Violence, 1994–2003," (report, National Institute of Justice, United States Department of Justice, Jerry Lee Center of Criminology, University of Pennsylvania, June 2004), http://1.usa.gov/100ypNc. • " 'rarely used in gun crimes even before the ban' " Christopher Koper with Daniel Woods and Jeffrey Roth, "An Updated Assessment of the Federal Assault Weapons Ban: Impacts on Gun Markets and Gun Violence, 1994–2003," (report, National Institute of Justice, United States Department of Justice, Jerry Lee Center of Criminology, University of Pennsylvania, June 2004), http://1.usa.gov/100ypNc. • " 'the assault weapon ban did not have an effect on firearm homicides' " Greg Ridgeway, Ph.D., "Summary of Select Firearm Violence Prevention Strategies," National Rifle Association Institute for Legislative Action, January 4, 2013, http://bit.ly/11hcPWb.

YOU ARE SO OUT OF TOUCH: EVEN THE MOST CONSERVATIVE MEMBER OF THE SUPREME COURT THINKS WE SHOULD BAN ASSAULT WEAPONS.

PAGE 43: "Scalia does not believe that the right to bear arms is absolute" Evan Puschak, "The NRA and its 'Tyranny Hypotheticals,' " tv.msnbc.com, January 23, 2013, http://on.msnbc.com/11hcNgT. • " 'And it's not very controversial that that's the case' " Rachel Maddow, Rachel Maddow Show, MSNBC, January 11, 2011, http://nbcnews.to/10jJxav. • "the sort not 'in common use' by the public can be regulated or banned" Ian Millhiser, "Rick Perry Falsely Claims an Assault Rifle Is Unconstitutional," thinkprogress.org, January 15, 2013, http://bit.ly/11hcKS7. • PAGE 44: " 'we do not undertake an exhaustive historical analysis today of the full scope of the Second Amendment' " District of Columbia, et al., Petitioners v. Dick Anthony Heller, 478 F. 3d 370 (D.C. 2008), http://bit.ly/IBGaj. • PAGE 45: " '[T]he Second Amendment does not protect those weapons not typically possessed by law-abiding citizens for lawful purposes' " District of Columbia v. Heller, 554 U.S. 570 (2008), http://1.usa.gov/11hczGu. • "is certainly not 'in common use' by the public" District of Columbia v. Heller, 554 U.S. 570 (2008), http://1.usa.gov/11hczGu. • PAGE 46: "There are about 4 million AR-15 rifles in America" Doug McKelway, "Dems Ramp Up Push for Assault Weapons Ban, Face Headwinds from States," foxnews.com, February, 28, 2013, http://fxn.ws/100Fb5D. • "82 percent of new handguns manufactured in the United States are semi-automatics" U.S. Department of Justice, Bureau of Alcohol, Tobacco, Firearms, and Explosives, Firearms Commerce in the United States 2011, (Washington, D.C. 2012), http://1.usa.gov/100Htl8.

NO CIVILIAN NEEDS A MILITARY STYLE WEAPON.

PAGE 46: " 'threatening our law enforcement officers' " President Barack Obama, "Remarks by the President on Preventing Gun Violence in Minneapolis, MN," Press Secretary, White House, February 4, 2013, http://1.usa.gov/100HwNO. • " 'to kill large numbers of people in close combat are replicated for civilian use' " Tommy Christopher, "Sen. Dianne Feinstein Holds Press Conference to Introduce New Assault Weapons Ban," mediaite.com, January 24, 2013, http://bit.ly/100HyoW. • " 'It's a military-style weapon' " Sen. Richard Blumenthal, Rachel Maddow Show, MSNBC, December 18, 2012, http://nbcnews.to/11hcvqg. • PAGE 47: " 'how they gather information to make 'well-informed' decisions' " Paul H. Thibodeau, Lera Boroditsky, "Metaphors We Think With: The Role of Metaphor in Reasoning," PloS One 6, No. 2 (February 23, 2011), http://bit.ly/100HCFk. • " 'it is much easier to justify why one

is against control than it is to justify why one is against safety' " Jonathon Schuldt, " 'Gun Control' of 'Gun Safety' the Battle Is Already Under Way," *newswise.com*, January 22, 2013, http://bit.ly/11hcwud. • **"Biden on gun safety: No more excuses"** Lucy Madison, "Biden on Gun Safety: No More Excuses," *cbsnews.com*, February 27, 2013, http://cbsn.ws/11hcsdX. • **"Debate over gun safety, rights comes home to Oakland County"** Bill Laitner, "Debate Over Gun Safety, Rights Comes Home to Oakland," *Detroit Free Press*, February 26, 2013, http://on.freep.com/100HDJq. • **PAGE 48: "Gun Safety Advocates Force NRA Backed Democrat Out Of Congressional Race"** Igor Volsky, "Gun Safety Advocates Force NRA Backed Democrat Out of Congressional Race" *thinkprogress.org*, February 18, 2013, http://bit.ly/100HF3P. • **"Biden Presses Senate Democrats to Support Gun Safety Agenda"** Jennifer Steinhauer, "Biden Presses Senate Democrats to Support Gun Safety Agenda," *Caucus* blog at *nytimes.com*, January 31, 2013, http://nyti.ms/100HFRz. • **"Chicago officials push for new gun safety legislation"** Karen Jordan, "Chicago Officials Push for New Gun Safety Legislation," *abc.go.local.com*, February 11, 2013, http://bit.ly/100HINf.

YEAH, BUT IF YOU MODIFY ONE, IT BECOMES FULLY AUTOMATIC.

PAGE 49: " 'These are killing machines. They are machine guns' " Piers Morgan, "NRA: Put Armed Guards in Schools," *Piers Morgan Tonight*, CNN, December 21, 2012, http://bit.ly/11haWIP.

I STILL DON'T UNDERSTAND WHY ANYONE WOULD NEED A SEMI-AUTOMATIC IN THEIR HOME.

PAGE 50: " 'unleash hundreds of shots in a matter of a few minutes and slaughter innocent Americans' " Piers Morgan, "Gun Control in America; Aurora Families Speak Out," *Piers Morgan Tonight*, CNN, December 17, 2012, http://bit.ly/11hckv3. • **PAGE 52:** " 'The intruders were met with armed resistance' " Tovin Lapan, "1 Dead, 3 at Large in Home Invasion at Apartment Complex," *Las Vegas Sun*, December 24, 2012, http://bit.ly/11hcgLR. • **"A home invasion robbery left one intruder dead and three other intruders injured"** Leticia Ordaz, "3 Wounded, One Intruder Dead in Sacramento Home Invasion," *kcra.com*, December 23, 2012, http://bit.ly/100HLbW. • **"A woman and her boyfriend arrived at her home to find several armed men inside"** "Intruder Killed Inside Home," *ProNews Channel 7, ABC*, http://bit.ly/11hciDp. • **"three men entered a home to commit a robbery"** Mike Morris, "Home Invasion Suspect Killed in Gunfight at DeKalb Apartment Complex," *Atlanta Journal-Constitution*, December 19, 2012,http://bit.ly/100HR3k. • **four people tried to break into the home of James Truman"** "Home Invasion Suspect Shot by Homeowner in Boardman," *foxyoungstown.com*, December 15, 2012, http://bit.ly/100HXaV. • **"firing 'multiple rounds' at three intruders who broke into his home"** Brooke Edwards Staggs, "Elderly Man Shoots at Intruders," *Victorville Daily Press*, December 8, 2012, http://bit.ly/11hcanq. • **"Three armed men broke into a house on a Monday morning"** Harry Harris and Katy Murphy, "Gunfire during attempted home invasion prompts lockdown at Oakland middle school," *San Jose Mercury News*, December 3, 2012, http://bit.ly/100I1aK.

I'VE HEARD THAT YOU PLAN ON DEFEATING THE ENTIRE UNITED STATES MILITARY WITH YOUR ASSAULT RIFLE.

PAGE 53: " 'Being able to kill U.S. soldiers' " Joe Scarborough, ".@3storybooks This is the survivalist argument that lies at the heart of the assault weapon defense—Being able to kill US soldiers." January 15, 2013, 8:05p.m., Twitter post, https://twitter.com/JoeNBC/status/291395640905310208. • **' 'which puts you in the difficult position of having to argue tyranny hypotheticals' "** Jon Stewart "Grand Theft Semi-Auto—Coming for Your Guns," *The Daily Show, Comedy Central*, January 17, 2013, http://bit

.ly/10jDVNp. • " 'not hyperbole if you believe the gun radicals' philosophy about guns' " Rachel Maddow, "You and me and the 82nd Airborne," *Rachel Maddow Show, MSNBC*, January 14, 2011, http://on.msnbc.com/10jE0R4. • **PAGE 56:** " 'killed 55 people, injured almost 2,000, led to 7,000 arrests' " "April 29, 1992: Riots Erupt in Los Angeles," *history.com*, accessed March 3, 2013, http://bit.ly/11hcbry. • " 'It's downtown Baghdad' " "Governor: Evac Superdome, Rescue Centers," *foxnews .com*, August 20, 2005, http://fxn.ws/10jE6bu. • " 'The looting is out of control. The French Quarter has been attacked' " "Governor: Evac Superdome, Rescue Centers," *foxnews.com*, August 20, 2005, http://fxn.ws/10jE6bu. • **PAGE 57:** "a man had a gun stuck in his face" Greg Wilson, "Man Pulls Gun in Gas Line, State Troopers Deployed at Stations as Tensions Boil in Sandy's Wake," *foxnews.com*, November 02, 2012, http://fxn.ws/10jEbM9. • " 'You see the worst in people at a time like this' " Greg Wilson, "Man Pulls Gun in Gas Line, State Troopers Deployed at Stations as Tensions Boil in Sandy's Wake," *foxnews.com*, November 02, 2012, http://fxn .ws/10jEbM9. • **"down with a handgun holding a maximum of seven rounds (which is now the limit in New York)"** Jessica Alaimo, "In Gun Law, Cuomo Mandated Something That Doesn't Exist," *democratanD.C.hronicle.com*, February 28, 2013, http://on.rocne.ws/10jEgQa.

I'M GLAD YOU BROUGHT THE SECOND AMENDMENT UP AGAIN. YOU HAVE TO ADMIT THAT IT'S PRETTY OUTDATED.

PAGE 57: " 'could carry an assault weapon' " "Dannel Malloy, Michael Bloomberg, Dianne Feinstein, Bill Bennett, David Brooks, Randi Weingarten, Tom Ridge, Michael Eric Dyson, Pete Williams," *Meet the Press*, NBC, December 16, 2012, http://nbcnews.to/11hc3s9. • "'The 2nd Amendment didn't take into account assault weapons' " "Put Armed Guards in Schools," *Piers Morgan Tonight*, CNN, December 21, 2012 http://bit.ly/11haWIP. • **PAGE 58:** " 'the Second Amendment does not give you the right to bear any kind of arm' " Ed Schultz, *Ed Show*, MSNBC, December 19, 2012, http://nbcnews.to/11hbUVz. • **PAGE 59: "a skilled printer could produce 250 sheets in two hours"** "Printing," Jacob Tonson, "Print Culture in Eighteenth-Century England: Printing," *umich.edu*, accessed March 3, 2013, http://bit.ly/11hbSgr. • **"produce 70,000 copies of an entire newspaper in an hour"** Bob Wilson, "How Newspapers Work," *howstuffworks.com*, accessed March 3, 2013, http://bit.ly/eZfP7y. • **PAGE 60: "and resulting in the deaths of at least seventeen people"** Dan Glaister and Declan Walsh, "After Week of Riots, Newsweek Admits It Got Qur'an Story Wrong," *Guardian*, May 16, 2005, http://bit.ly/11hbP4i. • **PAGE 61:** " 'handguns firing five to seven shots without reloading were in use by the end of the eighteenth century' " Clayton Cramer and Joseph Edward Olson, "Pistols, Crime, and Public: Safety in Early America," *Williamette Law Review* 44 (June 3, 2008), http://bit.ly/10jEtTp. • **"Guns were in hand and getting better with every generation"** Clayton Cramer and Joseph Edward Olson, "Pistols, Crime, and Public: Safety in Early America," *Williamette Law Review* 44 (June 3, 2008), http://bit.ly/10jEtTp. • **"for mass production of firearms (ten thousand units) using interchangeable parts"** "The Factory," *eliwhitney.org*, accessed March 3, 2013, http://bit.ly/YHb3do. • **"By the early nineteenth century, interchangeable parts were used routinely"** "Interchangeable Parts," *history.com*, accessed March 3, 2013, http://bit.ly/11hbKxs. • **"Firearms quickly became America's first mass-production export"** "Interchangeable Parts," *history.com*, accessed March 3, 2013, http://bit.ly/11hbKxs.

EVEN IF THAT'S TRUE, EVERYONE AGREED THAT THE SECOND AMENDMENT WAS ONLY ABOUT MILITIAS.

PAGE 62: " 'said individuals have a right to bear arms under the Second Amendment' " "Remembering Olivia Engel; Gun Control in America; Interview with Carolyn McCarthy, Ron Barber," *Piers Morgan Tonight*, CNN, December 18, 2012, http://bit.ly/11hag6p. • **PAGE 63:** " 'a well-regulated Militia' " David B. Kopel, "The Second Amendment in the Nineteenth Century," *BYU Law Review* 4 (1998), 1359–1554, http://bit.ly/Y84rv4. The Seventh Circuit Court of Appeals extolled this article as a model of "originalist interpretive method as applied to the Second Amendment." • **"The Amendment protects an 'individual' right"** *District of Columbia v. Heller*, 554 U.S. 570 (2008), http://bit.ly/rkyEKx. • **PAGE 64: "In other words, all nine justices, including those who were not, as Toobin put it, 'Republican appointees,' agreed that the Second Amendment protects some sort of individual right."** Note: The Stevens dissent argued that the Second Amendment also includes the collective right of the people in the States to have a militia. This approach rejected all of the lower court "collective right" cases, which had said that the existence of a collective right negates the existence of any individual right. The *Heller* majority did not explore the issue of whether the Second Amendment also includes State or collective rights, in addition to the individual right. • **"the state militia, in its official capacity and while in actual service, could not be disarmed"** *City of Salina v. Blaksley* 72 Kans. 230 (1905). • " 'to the collective body and not individual rights' " *U.S. v. Adams*, 11 F.Supp. 216 (S.D.Fla. 1935). • " 'as a protection for the States in the maintenance of their militia organizations"** *United States v. Tot*, 319 U.S 463 (1943). • **PAGE 65:** " 'collective right "of the people" to keep and bear arms in connection with "a well-regulated militia" ' " *Burton v. Sills*, 53 N.J. 86 (1968). • **"the Constitution guaranteed their individual right to own firearms"** Saul Cornell, "The Second Amendment Goes to Court," *Origins: Current Events in Historical Perspective* 1, no. 5 (February 2008), http://bit.ly/11hbz5j. • **PAGE 66:** " 'the right to keep and bear arms' " *Poe v. Ullman*, 367 U.S. 497 (1961), http://bit.ly/11lgupA. • **"quoted with approval in several subsequent Supreme Court cases"** *Planned Parenthood of Southeastern PA v. Casey*, 505 U.S. 833 (1992), http://bit.ly/GBmaxs. • **"in both the majority and the dissent in *Moore v. East Cleveland*"** *Moore v. East Cleveland*, 431 U.S. 494 (1977), http://bit.ly/11hbte2. • **"and in Justice Potter Stewart's concurrence in *Roe v. Wade*"** *Roe v. Wade*, 410 U.S. 113 (1973), http://bit.ly/11hbxuh.

MOST GUNS KEPT IN THE HOME ARE USED FOR SOMETHING OTHER THAN SELF-DEFENSE.

PAGE 67: " 'four accidental shootings, and 11 attempted or successful suicides' " "Dangerous Gun Myths," *New York Times*, February 2, 2013, http://nyti.ms/11hbrTc. • **"ask their relatives if a gun had been kept in the home"** Arthur L. Kellerman, Frederick P. Rivara, Norman B. Rushforth, and others, "Gun Ownership as a Risk Factor for Homicide in the Home," *New England Journal of Medicine* 329 (October 7, 1993), 1084–91, http://bit.ly/11hbmz0. • **"must have been the very same gun that was used in the killing"** Arthur L. Kellerman, Frederick P. Rivara, Norman B. Rushforth, and others, "Gun Ownership as a Risk Factor for Homicide in the Home," *New England Journal of Medicine* 329 (October 7, 1993), 1084–91, http://bit.ly/11hbmz0. • " 'noted that the gun involved had been kept in the home' " Arthur L. Kellerman, Frederick P. Rivara, Norman B. Rushforth, and others, "Correspondence: Gun Ownership as a Risk Factor for Homicide in the Home," *New England Journal of Medicine* 330, no. 5 (February 3, 1994), 366, 368, http://bit.ly/11hbnTw. • **PAGE 69: "were followed by criminals becoming more likely to attack people in their homes"** John R. Lott, Jr., and John E. Whitley, "Safe-Storage Gun Laws: Accidental Deaths, Suicides, and Crime," *Journal of Law and Economics* (October 2001), 659–89, http://bit.ly/10jFrPm. • **PAGE 70:** " 'no observable offsetting benefit in terms of reduced accidents or suicides' " John R. Lott, Jr., and John E. Whitley, "Safe-storage Gun Laws: Accidental Deaths, Suicides, and Crime," *Journal of Law and Economics* (October 2001), 659, http://bit.ly/10jFrPm. • **"there would be 355 more murders and almost**

5,000 more rapes" John R. Lott, Jr., and John E. Whitley, "Safe-storage Gun Laws: Accidental Deaths, Suicides, and Crime," *Journal of Law and Economics* (October 2001), 682, http://bit.ly/10jFrPm.

KEEPING A GUN AT HOME IS POINTLESS ANYWAY.

PAGE 71: " 'We are partners now. Can I count on you?' " Bruce Vielmetti, Steve Schultze, and Don Walker, "Sheriff David Clarke's Radio Ad Says 911 Not Best Option, Urges Residents to Take Firearms Classes," *Milwaukee Journal Sentinel*, January 25, 2013, http://bit.ly/10jG0J0. • **PAGE 72: "half the rate for victims who try to run away"** Gary Kleck and Don Kates, *Armed: New Perspectives on Gun Control* (New York: Prometheus Books, 2001), Table 7.1. • **"one-tenth the rate for those who did not try to protect themselves in any way"** John R. Lott Jr., More Guns, Less Crime, 3rd ed. (Chicago: University of Chicago, 2010). • " 'as well as a criminal's incentive to commit violent crimes and to be armed' " Lawrence Southwick Jr., "Self-Defense with Guns: The Consequences," *Journal of Criminal Justice* 28, no. 5 (September/ October 2000), 351–70.

OKAY, BUT THAT DOESN'T APPLY TO WOMEN. THEY'RE STILL MORE LIKELY TO BE KILLED WHEN THERE'S A GUN IN THE HOME.

PAGE 72: " 'no evidence that a gun in the home is protective for the woman' " Ruth Marcus, "The Phony Pro-gun Argument," *Washington Post*, January 31, 2013, http:// bit.ly/10jHuTE. • **PAGE 73: "all three criminals then fled the scene"** "Magnolia Mother Fires Back at Burglary Suspects," *kbtx.com*, January 26, 2013, http://bit .ly/10jHCma. • **"she pulled a gun and the attacker ran away"** "Robbery Suspect Pulls Knife, Clerk Pulls Gun," *fox6now.com*, January 10,2013, http://bit.ly/11hbePT. • **"She fired six shots, hitting him five times"** "Woman Hiding with Kids Shoots Intruder," *wsbtv.com*, January 4, 2013, http://bit.ly/11hbgY2. • **"she shot and wounded the man"** "Oklahoma Girl, 12, Shoot Suspected Burglar," *foxnews.com*, October 19, 2012, http://fxn.ws/11hba2C. • **PAGE 74: "than when resisting with a gun"** Lawrence Southwick Jr., "Self-Defense with Guns: The Consequences," *Journal of Criminal Justice* 8 (2000), Tables 5 and 6. Note: Problems exist with the National Crime Victimization Survey both because of its non-representative sample (for example, it weights urban and minority populations too heavily) and because it fails to adjust for the fact that many people do not admit to a law enforcement agency that they used a gun, even defensively. These problems make it difficult to rely too heavily on these estimates but, unfortunately, this survey is the only source of evidence on the way the probability of significant injury varies in relation to the level and type of resistance. • **"An additional woman carrying a concealed handgun reduces the murder rate"** John R. Lott, Jr., More Guns, Less Crime, 3rd ed. (Chicago: University of Chicago, 2010). • **PAGE 75: "4.6 percent of all murders (603) in 2010 involved wives being murdered by their husbands"** "Crime in the United States, 2010," U.S. Department of Justice, Federal Bureau of Investigation, accessed March 8, 2013, Table 10, http://1 .usa.gov/10jHMda. • **"Given the number of married women (about 63,150,000 million)"** U.S. Census Bureau, http://1.usa.gov/SEDWIG. • **"90 percent of adult murderers had previous criminal records"** U.S. Department of Justice, Bureau of Justice Statistics, *Murder in Large Urban Counties*, 1988 (Washington, D.C., 1993), http://1.usa.gov/WF59gg, See also: U.S. Department of Justice, *Murder in Families* (Washington, D.C., 1994), See also: Don B. Kates and Dan Polsby, "The Background of Murders" (working paper, Northwestern University Law School, Evanston, IL, 1997). Note: In these seventy-five largest counties in 1988, 77 percent of murder arrestees and 78 percent of defendants in murder prosecutions had criminal histories, with more than 13 percent of murders being committed by minors, who by definition cannot have criminal records. This implies that 89 percent of those arrested for murders must be adults with criminal records, with 90 percent of those being prosecuted. • "**a record of previous arrests for 'a major violent crime or burglary'**" Gary Kleck and David J. Bordua, "The Factual Foundation for Certain Key Assumptions of Gun Control," *Law and Policy Quarterly, Issue on Firearms and Firearms Regulation: Old Premises, New Research* 5, no. 3 (1983), http://bit.ly/11hb4s3. • "**represent only the tip of the iceberg'**" Gary Kleck and David J. Bordua, "The Factual Foundation for Certain Key Assumptions of Gun Control," *Law and Policy Quarterly, Issue on Firearms and Firearms Regulation: Old Premises, New Research* 5, no. 3 (1983), http://bit.ly/11hb4s3.

FORTY PERCENT OF ALL GUNS ARE SOLD WITHOUT BACKGROUND CHECKS.

PAGE 75: " '**It's not fair to responsible gun buyers or sellers'** " President Barack Obama, "Remarks by the President and the Vice President on Gun Violence," Office of the Press Secretary, the White House, January 16, 2013, http://1.usa.gov/10jIiI4. • **PAGE 76:** " '**40 percent of all gun trades, there's no background check'** " Piers Morgan, "NRA: Put Armed Guards in Schools," *Piers Morgan Tonight*, CNN, December 21, 2012, http://bit.ly/11haWIP. • " '**40 percent of gun sales now take place privately'** " "The Moment for Action on Guns," *New York Times*, January 14, 2013, http://nyti.ms/10jImrx. • "**It's been printed in the *New York Times*, *USA Today* and the *Wall Street Journal*** " Peter Baker and Michael Shear, "Obama to 'Put Everything I've Got' Into Gun Control," *New York Times*, January 16, 2013, http://nyti.ms/10jIqrl, See also: "Obama at the Gun Rack," *Wall Street Journal*, January 16, 2013, http://on.wsj.com/10jICH4, See also: "NRA Says Congress Will Not Pass Weapons Ban," *USA Today*, January 14, 2013, http://usat.ly/10jIEyz. • " '**no such screen on the person buying the gun'** " Chris Wallace, "Gun debate opponents gear up for fight," *Fox News Sunday*, Fox News, January 13, 2013, http://fxn.ws/10jIJCm. • " '**48 percent of gun sales'** " "Senate Judiciary Committee hearing on gun violence on Jan. 30, 2013 (transcript)," *Washington Post*, January 30, 2013,http://wapo.st/10jIOG7. • "**There's the first red flag: these numbers are nearly twenty years old**" Philip J. Cook and Jens Ludwig, U.S. Department of Justice, National Institute of Justice, *Guns in America: National Survey on Private Ownership and Use of Firearms*, (Washington, D.C., May 1997), http://1.usa.gov/QYSkvG. • **PAGE 77:** "**35.7 percent said they acquired it from someone other than a licensed dealer**" U.S. Department of Justice, National Institute of Justice, *The Police Foundation, National Study of Private Ownership of Firearms in the United States*, 1994, (Washington D.C., 1994). • "**researchers in some cases 'made a judgment call'** " "Kirsten Gillibrand Says 40 Percent of Guns Sold Today Escape Background Check," *politifact.com*, accessed March 8, 2013, http://bit.ly/10jIXcE. • "**even President Obama's background check proposal excludes gun transfers within a family**" Haughey, John, "Fact Check: Joe Biden's Interview on Gun Control and Universal Background Checks," March 8, 2013, http://bit.ly/10jJOoS. • **PAGE 78:** " '**plus or minus six percentage points'** " Glenn Kessler, "Update: Obama Claim on Background Checks Moved from 'Verdict Pending' to 2 Pinocchio's," *Fact Checker* blog at *washingtonpost.com*, January 25, 2013, http://wapo.st/10jJhbv. • "**there were more than 283,000 federally licensed gun dealers**" Bureau of Alcohol, Tobacco, Firearms, and Explosives, "Decline in the Number of Federal Firearms Licenses," atf.gov, June 2008, http://1.usa.gov/11haTN8. • "**while today there are just 118,000**" Bureau of Alcohol, Tobacco, Firearms, and Explosives, "Firearms Commerce in the United States," atf.gov, 2011, Exhibit 13, http://1.usa.gov/100Htl8. • **PAGE 79:** " '**The loophole is called the gun show loophole'** " Mayor Michael Bloomberg, *Meet the Press*, NBC, December 16, 2012, http://nbcnews.to/10jJkUL. • " '**We've got to end the gun show loophole'** " Mayor Cory Booker, *Rachel Maddow Show*, MSNBC, January 11, 2011, http://nbcnews.to/10jJxav. • " '**that's

40 percent of the sales in this country' " Ed Schultz, *Ed Show*, NBC, February 4, 2013, http://nbcnews.to/10jJsDG.

GUN SHOWS ARE WHERE CRIMINALS GET ALL THEIR WEAPONS.

PAGE 79: " 'there's no regulation, there's no background checks' " Mayor Cory Booker, *Rachel Maddow Show*, MSNBC, December 17, 2012, http://nbcnews.to/10jJBH8. • **PAGE 80:** " 'they were not even worth reporting as a separate figure' " Dave Kopel, "Will Gun Shows Become Extinct?" *America's 1st Freedom*, July 2010, http://bit.ly/101cJR3. • **Fewer than one percent of inmates (0.7 percent) who said they had a gun reported that they'd obtained it from a gun show"** Caroline Wolf Harlow, "Firearm Use by Offenders: Survey of Inmates in State and Federal Correctional Facilities," (report, Bureau of Justice Statistics, U.S. Department of Justice, Washington D.C., November 2011), http://bjs.ojp.usdoj.gov/content/pub/pdf/fuo.pdf. • **"not a single, credible academic study showing that these regulations reduce any type of violent crime"** John R. Lott, Jr., *The Bias Against Guns* (Washington, D.C., Regnery Publishing, Inc., 2003), 197.

EVEN A MAJORITY OF NATIONAL RIFLE ASSOCIATION MEMBERS SUPPORT UNIVERSAL BACKGROUND CHECKS.

PAGE 80: " 'asked NRA members earlier this year whether they support background checks on every gun sale, 74 percent agreed' " Arkadi Gerney, "All-American Carnage: Which Massacres to Remember? We Have Raised the Bloody Bar" *New York Daily News*, December 16, 2012, http://nydn.us/10jJKdF. • **PAGE 81:** " 'ending those secondary markets, makes a difference' " Mayor Cory Booker, "Guns in America," *Piers Morgan Tonight*, CNN, December 19, 2012, http://bit.ly/11haLgM. • " 'blocked 1.7 million prohibited individuals from buying a gun' " "Senate Judiciary Committee hearing on gun violence on Jan. 30, 2013 (transcript)," *Washington Post*, January 30, 2013, http://wapo.st/10jIOG7. • **"founded by gun-hating Mayors Bloomberg of New York City and Thomas Menino of Boston in 2006"** "Coalition History," *mayorsagainstallguns.org*, accessed March 9, 2013, http://maig.us/10jJR97. • **"The survey itself was conducted by Frank Luntz"** Frontline, "Interview: Frank Luntz," *pbs.org*, accessed March 9, 2013, http://to.pbs.org/10jJXh2. • **PAGE 82:** " 'repeatedly refused to make public essential facts about his research' " "AAPOR Finds Frank Luntz in Violation of Ethics Code," *aapor.org*, April 23, 1997, http://bit.ly/11haFG3. • " 'did not provide requested details about the poll's question wording' " Scott Clement, "NRA Members Strongly Oppose New Gun Restrictions, Poll Finds," *Washington Post*, January 25, 2013, http://wapo.st/10jJZFH. • " 'Internet panel to contact self-identified NRA members' " Scott Clement, "NRA Members Strongly Oppose New Gun Restrictions, Poll Finds," *Washington Post*, January 25, 2013, http://wapo.st/10jJZFH. • **PAGE 83:** " 'laws covering the sale of guns should be more strict' " The Word Doctors, *Gun Owners: NRA Gun-Owners & Non-NRA Gun-Owners*, (survey for Mayors Against Illegal Guns, The Word Doctors, Alexandria, VA, December 2009), http://maig.us/10jK8ZJ. • " 'federal law banning the sale of firearms between private citizens' " Wes Anderson "NRA National Member Survey Final," (survey, OnMessage Inc., Alexandria, VA, January 13–14, 2013), http://bit.ly/10jKcbQ.

THE NRA IS THE POSTER CHILD FOR BAD RESEARCH.

PAGE 83: " '[The NRA] only funds research that will lead to these conclusions' " Alan Dershowitz, "Mayor Bloomberg Speaks on Guns; The Right to Bear Arms; Acts of Heroism," *Piers Morgan Tonight*, CNN, July 23, 2012, http://bit.ly/11haz16. • " 'commissioning so-called scholars to come up with the kinds of lies' " Alan Dershowitz, "Gun Control in America," *Piers Morgan Tonight*, CNN, December 18, 2012, http://bit.ly/11hag6p. • **PAGE 84:** " 'RTC laws do in fact help drive down the murder rate' " James Q. Wilson, "Dissent," Appendix A, in *Firearms and Violence: A Critical Review*, eds. Charles F. Wellford, John V. Pepper and Carol V. Petrie (Atlanta, GA: National Academies Press, 2005), 271, http://bit.ly/YsppiD. • **"Attacks on . . . 'NRA funding,' regularly pop up in the gun control debate and are regularly debunked"** I think this shows how desperate gun control advocates can become in trying to destroy their opponents. On September 4, 1996 then Congressman, now Senator, Charles Schumer (D-NY) wrote the following in the *Wall Street Journal*:

> "I'd like to point out one other 'association.' The Associated Press reports that Prof. Lott's fellowship at the University of Chicago is funded by the Olin Foundation, which is 'associated with the Olin Corporation,' one of the nation's largest gun manufacturers. Maybe that's a coincidence, too. But it's also a fact."

Congressman Schumer's letter elicited a powerful response from William Simon, the Olin Foundation's president and former U.S. Treasury secretary, in the *Wall Street Journal* two days later. Here is an excerpt:

An Insult to Our Foundation

As president of the John M. Olin Foundation, I take great umbrage at Rep. Charles Schumer's scurrilous charge (Letters to the Editor, Sept. 4) that our foundation underwrites bogus research to advance the interests of companies that manufacture guns and ammunition. He asserts (falsely) that the John M. Olin Foundation is "associated" with the Olin Corp. and (falsely again) that the Olin Corp. is one of the nation's largest gun manufacturers. Mr. Schumer then suggests on the basis of these premises that Prof. John Lott's article on gun-control legislation (editorial page, Aug. 28) must have been fabricated because his research fellowship at the University of Chicago was funded by the John M. Olin Foundation.

This is an outrageous slander against our foundation, the Olin Corp., and the scholarly integrity of Prof. Lott. Mr. Schumer would have known that his charges were false if he had taken a little time to check his facts before rushing into print. Others have taken the trouble to do so. For example, Stephen Chapman of the *Chicago Tribune* looked into the charges surrounding Mr. Lott's study, and published an informative story in the Aug. 15 issue of that paper, which concluded that, in conducting his research, Prof. Lott was not influenced either by the John M. Olin Foundation or by the Olin Corp. Anyone wishing to comment on this controversy ought first to consult Mr. Chapman's article and, more importantly, should follow his example of sifting the facts before reaching a conclusion.

THE 2004 REPORT SAID WE NEED MORE DATA AND RESEARCH ON GUNS— AND THEY'RE RIGHT, WE NEED TO KNOW MORE.

PAGE 86: " 'the pervasiveness of guns in our society is destroying America' " Josh Feldman, "Piers Morgan and Alan Dershowitz Get in Shouting Match with Other Panelists Over Gun Control," *mediaite.com*, August 7, 2012, http://bit.ly/10jL3t0. • **"waiting periods, stand-your-ground laws, gun lock laws, and so on"** John R. Lott Jr., *More Guns, Less Crime*, 3rd ed. (Chicago: University of Chicago Press, 2010). • " 'mandated and funded by Congress and federal agencies' " "Who We Are," *nationalacademies.org*, accessed March 9, 2013, http://bit.ly/10jL7sT.

MORE GUNS MEANS MORE CRIME. ANY DATA TO THE CONTRARY IS A LIE OR NRA PROPAGANDA.

PAGE 87: " 'it makes us have a much more dangerous society' " Michael Bloomberg, *Meet the Press*, NBC, December 16, 2012, http://nbcnews.to/10jLa87. • "The NRA buys scholars. They buy statistics. It's just wrong' " Alan Dershowitz, "Guns in America," *Piers Morgan Tonight*, CNN, January 7, 2013, http://bit.ly/10jLcfY. • **PAGE 88:** "that clearly reduced violent crime, suicide or accidents" Charles F. Wellford, John V. Pepper and Carol V. Petrie, *eds., Firearms and Violence: A Critical Review* (Atlanta, GA: National Academies Press, 2005), http://bit.ly/TGJ6q3. • **PAGE 89:** "Per-Capita Firearm Murder Victims"** William J. Krouse, *Gun Control Legislation*, report prepared for Members and Committees of Congress, 112th Cong., 2d sess., 2012, Committee Print, 9, http://bit.ly/wvkslu. • **"Source of Firearm Estimate: 1994: Nat'l Inst. Of Justice"** Philip J. Cook and Jens Ludwig, U.S. Department of Justice, National Institute of Justice, *Guns in America: National Survey on Private Ownership and Use of Firearms* (Washington, D.C., May 1997), http://bit.ly/XqS6Mw. • **"Source of Firearm Estimate: 1996: ATF"** U.S. Department of the Treasury, Bureau of Alcohol, Tobacco and Firearms, *Commerce in Firearms in the United States* (Washington, D.C., February 2000), A3–A5. • **"Source of Firearm Estimate: 2000: ATF"** U.S. Department of the Treasury, Bureau of Alcohol, Tobacco and Firearms, *Firearms Commerce in the United States 2001/2002* (Washington, D.C., April 2002), E1–E3. • **"Source of Firearm Estimate: 2007: ATF"** U.S. Department of the Treasury, Bureau of Alcohol, Tobacco, Firearms, and Explosives, *Annual Firearm Manufacturing and Export Reports for 2002 through 2007* (Washington, D.C., May 2010). • **"Source of Firearm Estimate: 2011: ATF"** U.S. Department of the Treasury, Bureau of Alcohol, Tobacco, Firearms, and Explosives, *Firearms Commerce in the United States 2011* (Washington, D.C., August 2011), 11, 13, 15. • **PAGE 90:** "seems to point away from the premise that more guns leads to more crime, at least in Virginia. . . . From my personal point of view, I would say the data is pretty overwhelming."** Bowes, Mark, "Gun-related Violent Crimes Drop as Sales Soar in Va," *Richmond Times Dispatch*, January 28, 2013,http://bit.ly/10jM2tk. • **PAGE 91:** "bigger drops the longer the right-to-carry laws are in effect"** John R. Lott, Jr., *More Guns, Less Crime*, 3rd ed. (Chicago: University of Chicago Press, 2010), 10. • **"in a state without right-to-carry law sees a slight increase"** Stephen G. Bronars and John R. Lott, Jr., "Criminal Deterrence, Geographic Spillovers, and the Right to Carry Concealed Handguns," *American Economic Review* 88, no. 2 (1998), 475–79, See also: John R. Lott, Jr., *More Guns, Less Crime*, 3rd ed. (Chicago: University of Chicago Press, 2010). • **"violent crime relative to property crime"** Eric Helland and Alex Tabarrok, "Using Placebo Laws to Test 'More Guns, Less Crime,' " *Advances in Economic Analysis and Policy* 4, no. 1 (2004); see also: John R. Lott, Jr., *More Guns, Less Crime*, 3rd ed. (Chicago: University of Chicago Press, 2010). • **"murders relative to mass (multiple victim) public homicides"** John R. Lott, Jr., *The Bias Against Guns* (Washington, D.C., Regnery Publishing, Inc., 2003), Chapter 6. • **"studies have claimed either small benefits or no effect"** Bruce L. Benson and Brent D. Mast, "Privately Produced General Deterrence," *Journal of Law and Economics* 44, no. 2 (2001), 725, 734–35. • **PAGE 92:** " 'the longer a right-to-carry law is in effect, the greater the drop in crime' "** John R. Lott, Jr., and John E. Whitley, "Safe-Storage Gun Laws: Accidental Deaths, Suicides and Crime," *Journal of Law and Economics* 44, no. 2 (2001), 659, 680. • " 'concealed-handgun permit holders are extremely law abiding' "** John R. Lott, Jr., *More Guns, Less Crime*, 3rd ed. (Chicago: University of Chicago Press, 2010), 336. • " 'right-to-carry laws do help on average to reduce the number of these crimes' "** Florenz Plassmann and T. Nicolaus Tideman, "Does the Right to Carry Concealed Handguns Deter Countable Crimes? Only a Count Analysis Can Say," *Journal of Law and Economics* 44, no. 2

(2001), 771, 796. • " 'reinforce the basic findings of the original Lott and [David] Mustard study' " Carlisle E. Moody, "Testing for the Effects of Concealed Weapons Laws: Specification Errors and Robustness," *Journal of Law and Economics* 44, no. 2 (2001), 799–813. • " 'overall long run effect on crime' " Carlisle S. Moody and Thomas B. Marvell, "The Debate on Shall-Issue Laws" *Econ Journal Watch* 5, no. 3 (2008), 269, 292. • " 'crimes against persons and towards crimes against property' " Eric Helland and Alex Tabarrok, "Using Placebo Laws to Test 'More Guns, Less Crime,' " *Advances in Economic Analysis and Policy* 4, no. 1 (2004); see also: John R. Lott, Jr., *More Guns, Less Crime*, 3rd ed. (Chicago: University of Chicago Press, 2010). • " 'decrease in total homicides' driven by a drop in gun killings' " David E. Olsen and Michael D. Maltz "Right-to Carry Concealed Weapons Laws and Homicide in Large U.S. Counties: The Effect on Weapons Types, Victim Characteristics, and Victim-Offender Relationships," *Journal of Law and Economics* 44, no. 2 (2001), 747, 759. • " 'private security industry is rejected' " Bruce L. Benson and Brent D. Mast, "Privately Produced General Deterrence," *Journal of Law and Economics* 44, no. 2 (2001), 725, 734–35. • PAGE 93: "right-to-carry laws reduce violent crime" John R. Lott, Jr., *More Guns, Less Crime*, 3rd ed. (Chicago: University of Chicago Press, 2010), 283. • " 'no indication of any consistent RTC impact on crime' " Abhay Aneja, John J. Donohue III, and Alexandria Zhang, "The Impact of Right-to-Carry Laws and the NRC Report: Lessons for the Empirical Evaluation of Law and Policy," *American Law and Economics Review* 13, no. 2 (2011), 565, http://bit.ly/WF5lvX. • "severely biased the results toward finding a negative effect from right-to-carry laws" Carl Moody, John R. Lott, Jr., Thomas B. Marvell, and Paul R. Zimmerman, "Trust But Verify: Lessons for the Empirical Evaluation of Law and Policy" (working paper, College of William and Mary, Williamsburg, VA, January 25, 2012). • "A later addendum to this paper admitted the errors and claimed that the underlying results were still valid" Abhay Aneja, John J. Donohue III and Alexandria Zhang. "Addendum to 'The Impact of Right-to-Carry Laws and the NRC Report: Lessons for the Empirical Evaluation of Law and Policy,' " *American Law and Economics Review* 13, no. 2 (2011) http://bit.ly/WF5mjk. • "disagree, and have not been provided access to the data used to reach these conclusions" "Note on John Donohue's Latest Paper," John Lott's website, November 13, 2011, http://bit.ly/10jMCqR.

THE REASON NOTHING CHANGES IS THAT THE NRA BUYS OFF POLITICIANS.

PAGE 93: " 'trying to get exactly the measures in place that you've just suggested' " Piers Morgan, "Gun Control in America," *Piers Morgan Tonight*, CNN, December 20, 2012, http://bit.ly/11hag6p. . • PAGE 94: " 'Congress have an A-rating from the NRA' " Chris Wallace, "Captain Mark Kelly, Wayne LaPierre on Chances for Compromise in Gun Control Debate," *Fox News Sunday*, Fox News, February 3, 2013, http://fxn.ws/10jMGag. • "to protect our communities and our kids" President Barack Obama, "Remarks by the President and the Vice President on Gun Violence," Office of the Press Secretary, the White House, January 16, 2013, http://1.usa.gov/10jIiI4. • PAGE 95: " 'it's our fault, not the NRA's fault' " Alan Dershowitz, "Gun Control in America," *Piers Morgan Tonight*, CNN, January 7, 2013, http://bit.ly/10jLcfY. • "Do you think there should be a law banning the possession of handguns" "Guns," gallup.com, accessed March 10, 2013, http://bit.ly/ZM7ZPx. • PAGE 96: "illegal to manufacture, sell, or possess semi-automatic . . . assault rifles" "Guns," gallup.com, accessed March 10, 2013, http://bit.ly/ZM7ZPx. • "for context, the ACLU claims about 500,000 members" "ACLU History," *American Civil Liberties Union*, www.aclu.org/aclu-history. • "such as freedom of speech and freedom of the press" "Slim Majority of Americans Support Passing Stricter Gun Control Laws," August 15, 2012, http://bit.ly/11h99DE. • "The top recipients go $9,900" Michelle Martinelli and Michelle Merlin, "Gun Rights Groups' Political Spending Crushes That of Gun Control Supporters," *opensecrets.org*, December 14, 2012, http://bit.ly/11ha9Yx. • **PAGE 97:** "**or against Republicans who don't**" "AFL-CIO Outside Spending," *opensecrets.org*, accessed March 10, 2013, http://bit.ly/10jMTdA.

THE NRA IS SO CRAZY THAT THEY ACTUALLY WANT TO ARM OUR KIDS!

PAGE 97: " 'We don't want to live there' " Alan Dershowitz, "Guns in America," *Piers Morgan Tonight*, CNN, January 7, 2013, http://bit.ly/10jLcfY. • **PAGE 98:** " 'they can be deployed right now' " Wayne LaPierre, "The NRA Breaks Silence on Newtown Shooting," *CNN Newsroom*, CNN, December 21, 2012, http://bit.ly/10jN0FP. • "**federally funded by the Clinton administration**" Ashley Fantz, "NRA Clarifies Its Stance on Arming Schools," *cnn.com*, December 27, 2012, http://bit.ly/10jN4oY.

COLUMBINE PROVES THAT PUTTING ARMED GUARDS IN SCHOOLS JUST DOESN'T WORK.

PAGE 98: " '**were able to prevent the 15 deaths**' " "Michael Moore: Columbine's Armed Guards Were No Help," *twitchy.com*, December 21, 2012, http://bit.ly/10jNb4a. • " '**[Columbine] had armed guards and it didn't stop the tragedy**' " Ashley Fantz, "NRA Clarifies Its Stance on Arming Schools," *cnn.com*, December 27, 2012, http://bit.ly/10jN4oY. • **PAGE 99:** "**according to the Jefferson County, Colorado, Sheriff's Office**" "Jefferson County, Colorado, Sheriff: Deputies on Scene," *cnn.com*, accessed March 9, 2013, http://bit.ly/10jNgEW.

COLLEGE STUDENTS ARE TOO IRRESPONSIBLE TO CARRY GUNS.

PAGE 100: " 'We just don't need guns every place' " Michael Bloomberg, *Meet the Press*, NBC, December 16, 2012, http://nbcnews.to/10jNkEE. • **PAGE 101:** "**the right to carry concealed handguns on university campuses**" "Guns on Campus: Overview," *ncsl.org*, August 2012, http://bit.ly/11h8YrS. • "**most liberal universities have views similar to Mayor Bloomberg's**" Kate Murphy, "Most Professors Against Guns on College Campuses," *kentwired.com*, February 4, 2013, http://bit.ly/11h8JgG. • "**Florida issued permits to 2.4 million people**" "Concealed Weapon or Firearm License Summary Report, October 1, 1987–June 30, 2013," (report, Florida Department of Agriculture and Consumer Services Division of Licensing, Tallahassee, FL, 2003), http://bit.ly/11h8QZx. • "**the average person maintaining that permit for more than a decade**" John Lott, "Should Bans Against Carrying Concealed Weapons Be Lifted on College Campuses?" *foxnews.com*, March 9, 2011, http://fxn.ws/10jOWOL. • "**carrying a concealed handgun into a gun-free zone, such as a school or an airport**" Concealed Weapon or Firearm License Summary Report, October 1, 1987–June 30, 2013," (report, Florida Department of Agriculture and Consumer Services Division of Licensing, Tallahassee, FL, 2012), http://bit.ly/11h8QZx. • **PAGE 102:** "**there were 519,000 active license holders**" "Gun Control: States' Laws and Requirements for Concealed Carry Permits Vary across the Nation," (report, United States Government Accountability Office, Washington, D.C., July 2012), http://1.usa.gov/MPNBF6. • "**a rate of 0.023 percent—and only a few of those crimes involved a gun**" "Conviction Rates for Concealed Handgun License Holders, Reporting Period: 01/01/2011–12/31/2011" (report, Texas Department of Public Safety, Regulatory Services Division, Austin, TX, July 20, 2012), http://bit.ly/11h8G4y. • " '**pop a round at somebody**' " Bill Hallowell, "Campus Rape Victim Says Gun-Free Zones Empower Criminals, Defend Concealed Carry," *theblaze.com*, February 21, 2013, http://bit .ly/10jPi7O. • " '**I was in a safe zone and my attacker didn't care**' " Bill Hallowell, "Campus Rape Victim Says Gun-Free Zones Empower Criminals, Defend Concealed Carry," *theblaze.com*, February 21, 2013, http://bit.ly/10jPi7O.

THE POLICE SUPPORT MORE GUN CONTROL LAWS—YOU SHOULD, TOO.

PAGE 103: " 'we're going to go on strike [until more gun control is adopted]' " Michael Bloomberg, "Why Don't Police Stand Up," *Piers Morgan Tonight*, CNN, July 23, 2012, http://bit.ly/11gWqRw. • " '[should] be able to purchase a firearm for sport or self-defense' " National Association of Chiefs of Police and Sheriffs in the United States, "22nd Annual National Survey Questions," *nacoponline.org*, 2010, http://bit.ly/z84sm0. • **PAGE 104:** " 'crime-fighting potential of the professional law enforcement community' " National Association of Chiefs of Police and Sheriffs in the United States, "22nd Annual National Survey Questions," *nacoponline.org*, 2010, http://bit.ly/z84sm0. • " 'law would only be obeyed by law-abiding citizens' " David Griffith, "Shooting Straight: The Majority of Cops Believe Responsible Citizens Should Have the Right to Own Handguns," *Police: The Law Enforcement Magazine*, March 1, 2007, http://bit.ly/11gWMYr. • "**letting law-abiding private citizens carry concealed handguns**" San Diego Police Officers Association "Assault Weapons Survey Results," *Informant* newsletter, May 1997, http://bit.ly/11hOKOI. • "**especially if attacked by multiple assailants**" Kurtis Lee, "County Sheriffs of Colorado releases memo in opposition of new gun law," *Denver Post*, January 29, 2013, http://bit.ly/11gX15L.

WE SHOULD RESTRICT MAGAZIES TO A MAXIMUM OF TEN ROUNDS.

PAGE 104: " 'Why can't we ban assault weapons' " EJ Dionne, *Rachel Maddow Show*, MSNBC, January 13, 2011, http://nbcnews.to/11gXgh8. • **PAGE 105:** " 'only used for killing a large number of humans or trying to' " Rachel Maddow, *Rachel Maddow Show*, MSNBC, January 10, 2011, http://nbcnews.to/11gXkNO. • " 'at least restricting the size of the magazines to 10' " Rep. Jim Morgan, *Ed Show*, MSNBC, January 13, 2011, http://nbcnews.to/11gXpBg. • "**Or should it be seven bullets, as New York has decided**" David Ariosto, "N.Y. Governor Signs Nation's First Gun-Control Bill Since Newtown," *cnn.com*, January 28, 2013, http://bit.ly/11h8Atv. • "**three rounds**" Dianne Feinstein, *Congressional Record*, (July 29, 1993), Page: S9778, accessed March 18, 2013, http://1.usa.gov/ZydQJ7. • **PAGE 106:** "**they looked at involved magazines holding more than ten bullets**" Mark Follman and Gavin Aronsen, " 'A Killing Machine': Half of All Mass Shooters Used High-Capacity Magazines," *Mother Jones*, January 30, 2013, http://bit.ly/11h8vGg. • **PAGE 107:** "**forcing the others to flee**" "Family Fights Back When 3 Gunmen Storm Their Home; One Intruder Shot," *khou.com*, February 22, 2013, http://bit.ly/11gXzbA.

DON'T BELIEVE THE GUN NUTS: HITLER DIDN'T TAKE ANYONE'S FIREARMS AWAY.

PAGE 108: "**Hitler in fact relaxed gun control laws**" Backell, "Beware of Tyrants in Sheep's Clothing," *dailykos.com*, January 20, 2013, http://bit.ly/11gXHrB. • "**disarming opponents in order to prevent resistance**" Daniel D. Polsby and Don B. Kates Jr., "Of Holocausts and Gun Control," *Washington University Law Review* 75, no. 3 (1997), 1236–75, http://bit.ly/11gXMLU. • **PAGE 109:** " 'licenses to obtain or to carry firearms shall only be issued to persons whose reliability is not in doubt' " Jay Simkin and Aaron Zelman, *Gun Control: Gateway to Tyranny* (Milwaukee, WI: Jews for the Preservation of Firearms Ownership, Inc., 1992), 14, 52. • "**authorized the German states to register all firearms**" Jay Simkin and Aaron Zelman, *Gun Control: Gateway to Tyranny* (Milwaukee, WI: Jews for the Preservation of Firearms Ownership, Inc., 1992), 40. • " '**emergency decree**' " Stephen P. Halbrook, " 'Arms in the Hands of Jews Are a Danger to Public Safety': Nazism, Firearm Registration, and the Night of the Broken Glass," *St. Thomas Law Review* 21 (2009), 109, 123, http://bit.ly/11gXTqX. • " '**fall into the hands of radical elements**' " Stephen P. Halbrook, " 'Arms in the Hands of Jews Are a Danger to Public Safety': Nazism, Firearm Registration, and the Night of the Broken Glass," *St. Thomas Law Review* 21 (2009), 124, http://bit.ly/11gXTqX. • " 'was consolidated by massive searches and seizures of firearms from political opponents' " Stephen P. Halbrook, "Nazi Firearms Law and the Disarming of the German Jews," *Arizona Journal of International and Comparative Law* 17, no. 3 (2000), 483–84, http://bit.ly/11h8kuH. • **PAGE 110**: " 'Decree of the Reich President for the Protection of People and State' emergency measure" Otis C. Mitchell, *Hitler Over Germany: The Establishment of the Nazi Dictatorship (1918–1934)* (Ann Arbor, MI: Institute for the Study of Human Issues, 1983). • "**Nazi police began to search homes and offices for subversive literature and firearms**" "Red Terror Plans Alleged by Reich," *New York Times*, March 1, 1933. • "**searched 'for hidden arms, but found only a revolver' ** " "Nazis Raid Home of President Ebert's Widow," *New York Times*, March 15, 1933. • " 'but the nearest thing to arms they found was a bread knife' " "Nazis Hunt Arms in Einstein Home," *New York Times*, March 21, 1933. • " 'Nazi auxiliaries raided a Jewish quarter in Eastern Berlin' " "Raid on Jewish Quarter," *New York Times*, April 5, 1933. • **PAGE 111**: "Communist literature, arms, and munitions were seized in Berlin" "Seize Literature and Arms," *New York Times*, April 13, 1933. • " 'permits to carry arms will not in the future be issued to any member thereof' " "Permission to Possess Arms Withdrawn from Breslau Jews," *New York Times*, April 23, 1933. • **PAGE 112**: "as the state determined that you were not a threat" Stephen P. Halbrook, "Nazi Firearms Law and the Disarming of the German Jews," *Arizona Journal of International and Comparative Law* 17, no. 3 (2000), 513–14, http://bit.ly/11h8kuH. • "relying on those helpful Weimar firearm registration lists " Stephen P. Halbrook, " 'Arms in the Hands of Jews Are a Danger to Public Safety': Nazism, Firearm Registration, and the Night of the Broken Glass," *St. Thomas Law Review* 21 (2009), 115–22, http://bit.ly/11gXTqX. • "shops were ransacked and synagogues were burned" "Nazis Smash, Loot, and Burn Jewish Shops and Temples Until Goebbels Calls Halt," *New York Times*, November 11, 1938. • " 'are threatened with the severest punishment' " "Nazis Ask Reprisal in Attack on Envoy," *New York Times*, November 9, 1938. • **PAGE 113**: " 'penalty of twenty years confinement in a concentration camp' " "Possession of Weapons Barred," *New York Times*, November 11, 1938. • **PAGE 114**: " 'to retain possession of firearms—all these things are prohibited' " "Topics of the Times: Their Common Fate," *New York Times*, July 2, 1940. • "The most foolish mistake we could possibly make would be to allow the subject races to possess arms" Adolf Hitler, *Hitler's Secret Conversations, 1941–1944*, trans. Norman Cameron and RH Stevens (New York: Farrar Straus and Young,1961), 403.

PART TWO: WINNING HEARTS AND MINDS

PAGE 116: "before taking a stolen handgun out of his backpack and opening fire" Daniel Pederson, "Tragedy in a Small Place," *Newsweek*, December 14, 1997, http://thebea.st/11gYuZQ. • " 'And then I woke up' " Rick Bragg, "Forgiveness, After 3 Die in Shootings in Kentucky," *New York Times*, December 3, 1997, http://nyti.ms/11gYn09. • " 'Kill me, please' " Julie Grace and West Paducah, "When Silence Fell," *Time*, June 24, 2001, http://ti.me/11h8emA. • **PAGE 117**: "register a hit with only 20 percent of their shots from seven yards" Lt. Col. Dave Grossman and Gloria Degaetano, *Stop Teaching Our Kids to Kill: A Call to Action Against TV, Movie, and Video Game Violence* (New York: Crown Publishers, 1999), 4. • "this ninth-grade boy had never fired a real pistol before" Daniel Pederson, "Tragedy in a Small Place," *Newsweek*, December 14, 1997, http://thebea.st/11gYuZQ. • "modeled after a similar scene in the movie *Basketball Diaries*" Donald P. Baker, "As Kentucky Town Mourns, Movie Suggested as Basis for Boy's Attack," *Washington Post*, December 6,1997, http://wapo.st/11h826W. • "The book? *Rage*, by Stephen King" Stephen King, *Guns* (New York: Kindle Singles, 2013), Kindle edition. • **PAGE 118**:

"**fewer than 10 percent of lifelong smokers will ever get lung cancer**" Christopher Wanjek, "Smoking's Many Myths Examined," *livescience.com*, November 18, 2008, http://bit.ly/11h88M3. • **PAGE 121: "move up the ranks of a criminal organization**" Rockstar Games, *Information*, Take-Two Interactive Software, Inc., 2008, http://bit.ly/11gYLvM. • **PAGE 122:** " '**may lead to increased aggressive behavior in certain subgroups of children** ' " Surgeon General's Scientific Advisory Committee on Television and Social Behavior, *Television and Growing Up: The Impact of Televised Violence: Report to the Surgeon General*, U.S. Public Health Service, Washington, D.C.: U.S. Government Printing Office, 1972. • " '**motivated by violent video games**' " "Sandy Hook Shooter Adam Lanza Blacked Out Game Room, Bedroom," *CBS News*, February 19, 2013, http://cbsn.ws/11gYPLP. • **PAGE 123:** " '**was him and that TV screen with his tactical shooting game**' " "Sandy Hook Shooter Adam Lanza Blacked Out Game Room, Bedroom," *cbsnews.com*, February 19, 2013, http://cbsn.ws/11gYPLP. • **Or something you learn playing kill games**" Mike Lupica, "Lupica: Morbid find suggests murder-obsessed gunman Adam Lanza plotted Newtown, Conn.'s Sandy Hook massacre for years," *New York Daily News*, March 17, 2013, http://nydn.us/YsqXcr. • **PAGE 124:** " '**rack up the most kills—and played it every afternoon**' " "Anatomy of a Massacre," *Newsweek*, May 2, 1999, http://thebea .st/11gYRU8. • " '**hey it's just a game,' I say 'I don't care.'** ' " Jefferson County Sheriff's Office, "Columbine Documents: JC-001–025923 Through JC-001–026859," (report, Jefferson County Sheriff's Office, Golden, CO, January 8, 2003), 272, http://bit .ly/11gYXer. • "**spent most of his time playing video games**" Larry Bell, "Irrational Gun Rights Won't Prevent Senseless Violence," *Forbes*, December 23, 2012, http:// onforb.es/11gYZ60. • " '**i know how to cut a body open and eat you for more then a week. ;-)**' " Alexandra Berzon, John R. Emshwiller, and Robert A. Guth, "Postings of a Troubled Mind: Accused Shooter Wrote on Gaming Site of His Job Woes, Rejection by Women," *Wall Street Journal*, January 12, 2001, http://on.wsj.com/11gZ89G. • "**he liked to play Quake and Doom—two violent video games**" John Cloud/Springfield, "Of Arms and the Boy," *Time*, June 24, 2001, http://ti.me/11gZbSU. • " '**Everybody's got to die sometime**' " Rebecca Leung, "Can a Video Game Lead to Murder?" *CBS News*, February 11, 2009, http://cbsn.ws/11h7VYZ. • "**he appeared to have reenacted a scene from the game**" Rebecca Leung, "Can a Video Game Lead to Murder?" *CBS News*, February 11, 2009, http://cbsn.ws/11h7VYZ. • "**killing one person and seriously wounding another**" "Grand Theft Auto Comes Under Fire," *BBC News*, May 4, 2004, http://news.bbc.co.uk/2/hi/uk_news/scotland/3680481.stm. • " '**recreate scenes from the cult game [*Grand Theft Auto*]**' " Martyn Leek, "The Murder Rampage Game for Kids," *Sunday Mercury*, January 4, 2004, http://bit.ly/11gZhKb. • **PAGE 125: "the boy was stopped before anyone was hurt**" Jack Thompson, "More Columbines," *Washington Times*, July 1, 2004, http://bit.ly/11gZnBw. • " '**He played them too much, I am embarrassed to say**' " Jack Thompson, "More Columbines," *Washington Times*, July 1, 2004, http://bit.ly/11gZnBw.

SOMETHING IS DIFFERENT

PAGE 125: " '**most heavily armed people in the world**' " John Morgan Dederer, *War in America to 1775: Before Yankee Doodle* (New York: New York University Press, 1990), 116. • "**homicides involving guns were 'rare'** ' " Roger Lane, *Murder in America: A History* (Columbus, OH: Ohio State University Press, 1998), 59–60. • " '**the murder rate declined 27.7 percent**' " Don B. Kates and Gary Mauser, "Would Banning Firearms Reduce Murder and Suicide?" *Harvard Journal of Law and Public Policy* 30, no. 2 (Spring 2007), 685, http://hvrd.me/11gZvkC. • **PAGE 126: "the United States experienced its first double homicide in a school**" Katherine Ramsland, "School Killers,"*Crime Library* at *trutv.com*, accessed March 2, 2013, http://bit.ly/11h7SMQ. • "**where a juvenile committed a multiple homicide in a school prior to 1975**"

Wikipedia, "School Shooting," accessed March 8, 2013, http://en.wikipedia.org/wiki/School_shooting. • **PAGE 127: "he killed fifteen people at his high school"** "German school gunman 'kills 15,' " *BBC News*, March 11 2009, http://news.bbc.co.uk/2/hi/europe/7936817.stm. • **"he was an avid video game player"** "Teen Killer's Victims Mourned," *news24.com*, March 21, 2009, http://n24.cm/11gZywy. • **PAGE 128: " 'battle each other to the death' "** "Brave Teacher Stopped Gun Rampage," *cnn.com*, April 27, 2002, http://bit.ly/11gZA7Q. • **"a fourteen-year-old murdered two of his fellow students in his school in Rauma"** "School Shootings Rare in Finland," *yle.fi*, July 11, 2007, http://bit.ly/11gZEUU. • **"in Tuusula, an eighteen-year-old student murdered eight classmates in his high school"** "School Shootings Rare in Finland," *yle.fi*, July 11, 2007, http://bit.ly/11gZEUU. • **"a twenty-two-year-old student murdered ten people at Seinäjoki University"** Attila Cser, " Gunman Kills 10, Self in Finnish School Shooting," *reuters.com*, September 23, 2008, http://reut.rs/11gZLzV. • **"two people were murdered by a student at Monash University in Australia"** "Two People Shot Dead, Five Wounded at Monash Uni," *smh.com.au*, October 21, 2002, http://bit.ly/11gZOf5. • **"Two more were murdered by a seventeen-year-old student in his school in Thailand"** "Schoolyard Killings: Second student dies; security beefed up," *thenationmultimedia.com*, accessed March 2, 2013, http://bit.ly/11gZPQg. • **"Four people were killed by a fifteen-year-old student in their Argentina high school"** "4 Die in Argentina School Shooting," *cbsnews.com*, February 11, 2009, http://cbsn.ws/11h7NZN. • **"a former student returned to his old middle school with two .38-caliber revolvers"** Jeff Fick and John Lyons, "Rio Shooter Kills at Least 12 Young Students," *Wall Street Journal*, April 8, 2011, http://on.wsj.com/11gZWeH. • **PAGE 128: "murdered sixty-nine people and injured at least 110"** Australian Associated Press, "Norway Marks Anniversary of Twin Attacks that Claimed 77 Lives," *Herald Sun*, April 23, 2012, http://nyti.ms/11gZXiH. • **"In the year before the massacre, he would play World of Warcraft and Call of Duty extensively, sometimes up to sixteen hours a day"** Paul Goodman, "Norwegian Mass Murderer Defends Gaming Habits," *escapistmagazine.com*, April 19, 2012, http://bit.ly/11gZZqE.

DENYING THE SCIENCE

PAGE 129: " 'there is a cause-and-effect relationship between media violence and real-life violence' " American Academy of Pediatrics: Committee on Communications, "Media Violence," *Pediatrics* 95, no. 6 (June 1, 1995), 949–51, http://bit.ly/11h0mBK. • **"American children ages two to eleven see the first hour of prime-time shows on weekday evenings"** JT Hamilton, *Channeling violence: The economic market for violent television programming*, (Princeton, NJ: Princeton University Press, 1998). • **"American children under eight years old spend an average of two hours and fourteen minutes a day consuming digital media and television,"** Common Sense Media, *Zero to Eight: Children's Media Use in America* (San Francisco: Common Sense Media, Inc., 2011), http://www.commonsensemedia.org/sites/default/files/research/zerotoeightfinal2011.pdf. • **PAGE 130: " 'Nonviolent video game play also did not predict higher levels of aggressive behavior over time' "** T. Willoughby, PJ Adachi, and M. Good, "A Longitudinal Study of the Association Between Violent Video Game Play and Aggression Among Adolescents," (study, Department of Psychology, Brock University, St. Catharines, Ontario, Canada, 2012); http://www.ncbi.nlm.nih.gov/pubmed/22040315. • **"virtually mimic what has been found in other longitudinal studies"** Douglas A. Gentile, *Media Violence and Children* (Westport, CT: Praeger, November 30, 2003), 69–70. • **PAGE 131: "there have been thousands of studies performed and opinions issues over the last half century"** Lt. Col. Dave Grossman and Gloria Degaetano, *Stop Teaching Our Kids to Kill: A Call to Action Against TV, Movie and Video Game Violence* (New York: Crown Publishers, 1999), 132–36. • **PAGE 133: " 'it is the single most easily remediable contributing factor' "**

American Academy of Pediatrics: Committee on Communications, "Media Violence," *Pediatrics* 95, no. 6 (June 1, 1995), 949–51, http://bit.ly/WW2Vv3.

STIMULUS/RESPONSE

PAGE 134: "youth had witnessed an average of 200,000 acts of violence on television by age eighteen" Aletha C. Huston, Edward Donnerstein, Halford Fairchild, and others, *Big World, Small Screen: The Role of Television in American Society* (Lincoln, NE: University of Nebraska Press, 1992). • " **'media consumption among youth in the psychiatric population is 6 hours per day'** " Matt DeLisi, Michael G. Vaughn, Douglas A. Gentile, and others, "Violent Video Games, Delinquency, and Youth Violence: New Evidence," *Youth Violence and Juvenile Justice* 10, no. 4 (October 17, 2012). • **PAGE 135: "They quickly learn that violence is an acceptable solution"** Aletha C. Huston, Edward Donnerstein, Halford Fairchild, and others, *Big World, Small Screen: The Role of Television in American Society* (Lincoln, NE: University of Nebraska Press, 1992). • **"determine if those who'd played the violent games would be more aggressive"** Christopher R. Englehardt, Bruce D. Bartholow, Geoffrey T. Kerr, and others, "This Is Your Brain on Violent Video Games: Neural Desensitization to Violence Predicts Increased Aggression Following Violent Video Game Exposure," *Journal of Experimental Social Psychology* 47, no. 5 (September 20011), 1033–36. • **PAGE 136: " 'predicted an increase in aggression' "** Christopher R. Englehardt, Bruce D. Bartholow, Geoffrey T. Kerr, and others, "This Is Your Brain on Violent Video Games: Neural Desensitization to Violence Predicts Increased Aggression Following Violent Video Game Exposure," *Journal of Experimental Social Psychology* 47, no. 5 (September 20011), 1033–36. • **"we can 'detox' a child in a couple of days just by turning off the TV and video games"** Lt. Col. Dave Grossman, personal communication. • " **'young adults showed less activation in certain frontal brain regions following a week of playing violent video games at home' "** "Violent Video Games Alter Brain Function in Young Men," *Medical School News* at *indiana.edu*, December 1, 2011, http://bit.ly/11h0uB6. • " **'are important for controlling emotion and aggressive behavior' "** Violent Video Games Alter Brain Function in Young Men," *Medical School News* at *indiana.edu*, December 1, 2011, http://bit.ly/11h0uB6. • " **'effects may translate into behavioral changes over longer periods of game play' "** Violent Video Games Alter Brain Function in Young Men," *Medical School News* at *indiana .edu*, December 1, 2011, http://bit.ly/11h0uB6.

THE TRUTH ABOUT (NO) CONSEQUENCES

PAGE 137: " 'points are awarded for the murder of female prostitutes' " Lt. Col. Dave Grossman and Gloria Degaetano, *Stop Teaching Our Kids to Kill: A Call to Action Against TV, Movie and Video Game Violence* (New York: Crown Publishers, 1999), 70. • **"(and actually *was* banned in Australia)"** Tony Smith, "Australia Bans Manhunt," *theregister.co.uk*, September 30, 2004, http://bit.ly/11h2rxx. • " **'sticking axes into dudes, etc. It's all really standard fare, actually' "** Josh Wanamaker, "14 Most Offensive Video Games Ever," *gameranx.com*, September 28, 2012, http://bit.ly/11h2wkT. • **PAGE 138: "Grossman's *Stop Teaching Our Kids to Kill*"** Lt. Col. Dave Grossman and Gloria Degaetano, *Stop Teaching Our Kids to Kill: A Call to Action Against TV, Movie and Video Game Violence* (New York: Crown Publishers, 1999). • **"Josh Wanamaker of Gameranx.com"** Josh Wanamaker, "14 Most Offensive Video Games Ever," *gameranx.com*, September 28, 2012, http://bit.ly/11h2wkT. • **PAGE 139: "games that allow the player to be the killers in horrific real-life events"** Josh Wanamaker, "14 Most Offensive Video Games Ever," *gameranx.com*, September 28, 2012, http://bit .ly/11h2For. • **PAGE 140: " 'a "reward" for youth to spend their free time, it can be problematic' "** Matt DeLisi, Michael G. Vaughn, Douglas A. Gentile, and others,

"Violent Video Games, Delinquency, and Youth Violence: New Evidence," *Youth Violence and Juvenile Justice* 10, no. 4 (October 17, 2012).

TRAINED TO KILL

PAGE 141: " 'The violence in games hadn't prepared them for this' " Jose Antonio Vargas, "Virtual Reality Prepares Soldiers for Real War," *Washington Post*, February 14, 2006, http://wapo.st/11h2Lwd. • "in World War II only 15–20 percent of individual riflemen fired their weapons in close combat" Lt. Col. Dave Grossman, *On Killing: The Psychological Cost of Learning to Kill in War and Society* (New York: Back Bay Books, 2009), 36. • PAGE 142: "to 55 percent in Korea, to upwards of 95 percent since Vietnam" Lt. Col. Dave Grossman, *On Killing: The Psychological Cost of Learning to Kill in War and Society* (New York: Back Bay Books, 2009), 36. • "spent $1 billion on games technology that gets soldiers combat ready" "Moving to the Dark Side of the Screen," *Sydney Morning Herald*, May 13, 2006, http://bit.ly/11h2PMx. • " 'combat simulators [are] . . . the fastest way to train troops and the easiest way to save money' " "Moving to the Dark Side of the Screen," *Sydney Morning Herald*, May 13, 2006, http://bit.ly/11h2PMx. • " 'the U.S. Army has created their own violent video game as a recruitment tool' " Douglas A. Gentile, *Media Violence and Children* (Westport, CT: Praegar, November 30, 2003), 136. • PAGE 143: " 'This is simply astounding [for an untrained gunman]' " Lt. Col. Dave Grossman, "Statement of Lt. Col. Dave Grossman Before the New York State Legislature, October 1999," *thefreeradical.ca*, accessed March 3, 2013, http://bit.ly/11h2XeZ. • PAGE 144: " 'This is what should be expected from an untrained shooter' " Lt. Col. Dave Grossman, "Statement of Lt. Col. Dave Grossman Before the New York State Legislature, October 1999," *thefreeradical.ca*, accessed March 3, 2013, http://bit.ly/11h2XeZ. • " 'behaviors that could only have been learned in a video game' " Lt. Col. Dave Grossman, "Statement of Lt. Col. Dave Grossman Before the New York State Legislature, October 1999," *thefreeradical.ca*, accessed March 3, 2013,http://bit.ly/11h2XeZ. • " 'they did that naturally because the violent shooting game they played rewarded head shots' " Bradley Cornelius, "Dr. Brad Bushman, Ohio State University—Video Games and Shooting Skill," *wamc.org*, July 19, 2012, http://bit.ly/11h7spY. • "who reportedly shot his own mother several times in the head" Lt. Col. Dave Grossman, *On Killing: The Psychological Cost of Learning to Kill in War and Society* (New York: Back Bay Books, 2009), 128. • PAGE 145: "the 'Fire Arms Training Simulator' is . . . similar to the violent video game *Time Crisis*" Lt. Col. Dave Grossman and Gloria Degaetano, *Stop Teaching Our Kids to Kill: A Call to Action Against TV, Movie and Video Game Violence* (New York: Crown Publishers, 1999), 66. • " 'You have no choice but to shoot him and hope for the best' " Alan Feuer, "Ready, Aim, Ready?" *New York Times*, December 8, 2012, http://nyti.ms/11h3766. • " 'and unless you do scenario and role-play training, they're not going to have the experience to fall back on' " Alan Feuer, "Ready, Aim, Ready?" *New York Times*, December 8, 2012, http://nyti.ms/11h3766. • PAGE 146: "admitted that *Rage* was known to each of these killers . . . was a 'possible accelerant' " Stephen King, *Guns* (New York: Kindle Singles, 2013), Kindle edition. • " '[the book's main character] had to go. He was dangerous' " Stephen King, *Guns* (New York: Kindle Singles, 2013), Kindle edition. • " 'America's so-called culture of violence plays a significant role in kid-on-kid school shootings' " Stephen King, *Guns* (New York: Kindle Singles, 2013), Kindle edition.

SCAPEGOATING AND EXCUSES

PAGE 147: " 'America's propaganda-savvy gun pimps' " Stephen King, *Guns* (New York: Kindle Singles, 2013), Kindle edition. • " 'In video gaming, shooters still top the lists' " Stephen King, *Guns* (New York: Kindle Singles, 2013), Kindle edition. • " ' it is likely to be one of the most viewed of all entertainment experiences in modern history' " "Call of Duty® Franchise Surpasses $3 Billion in Retail Sales Worldwide," *prnewswire.com*, November 27, 2009, http://prn.to/11h3eP5. • **PAGE 148:** "It took just forty-two days for the title to gross $1 billion" Manikandan Raman, "Call of Duty: Black Ops Sales Top $1 Bln," *International Business Times*, December 22, 2010, http://bit.ly/11h3vkX. • **"more than 600 million hours had been logged playing the game in its first six weeks alone"** Manikandan Raman, "Call of Duty: Black Ops Sales Top $1 Bln," *International Business Times*, December 22, 2010, http://bit.ly/11h3vkX. • **"Xbox users log on more than once a day and play for more than an hour each time"** Manikandan Raman, "Call of Duty: Black Ops Sales Top $1 Bln," *International Business Times*, December 22, 2010, http://bit.ly/11h3vkX. • **"took just *sixteen days* to gross $1 billion"** Christopher Freeburn, " 'Call of Duty' Sales Top Hollywood's Highest Grossers," *investorplace.com*, December 6, 2012, http://bit.ly/11h4yRZ. • " **'exceeded worldwide ticket sales' "** Christopher Freeburn, " 'Call of Duty' Sales Top Hollywood's Highest Grossers," *investorplace.com*, December 6, 2012, http://bit.ly/11h4yRZ. • " **'guns are for bad guys too cowardly to fight like men' "** Stephen King, *Guns* (New York: Kindle Single, 2013), Kindle edition. • **"if you look at the top twenty instead, you find *Django Unchained* and *Taken 2***" "2012 Domestic Grosses," *boxofficemojo.com*, accessed March 3, 2013, http://bit.ly/IEETuB. • **PAGE 149:** **"The killer even dyed his hair to match The Joker's"** Richard Esposito, Jack Date, and Pierre Thomas, "Aurora 'Dark Knight' Suspect James Holmes Said He 'Was the Joker': Cops," *The Blotter* blog at abcnews.go.com, July 20, 2012, http://abcn.ws/11h7bmR. • **"*The Hunger Games* (the third-highest-grossing film in the U.S. in 2012)"** "2012 Domestic Grosses," *boxofficemojo.com*, accessed March 4, 2013, http://bit.ly/IEETuB. • " **'directed at people who have already expired' "** Stephen King, *Guns* (New York: Kindle Singles, 2013), Kindle edition. • **PAGE 151:** " **'with a rifle slung across the shoulder' "** Helena Bachmann, "The Swiss Difference: A Gun Culture that Works," *Time*, December 20, 2012, http://ti.me/11h4LEN. • **"Switzerland experiences about 0.5 gun homicides per 100,000 people annually"** Helena Bachmann, "The Swiss Difference: A Gun Culture that Works," *Time*, December 20, 2012, http://ti.me/11h4LEN. • **"The rate in the United States is about six times higher"** William J. Krouse, *Gun Control Legislation*, report prepared for Members and Committees of Congress, 12 Cong., 2d sess., 2012, Committee Print, 9,http://bit.ly/wvkslu. • **"concluded that a 'culture of support,' rather than focus on individualism, can deter mass killings"** Helena Bachmann, "The Swiss Difference: A Gun Culture that Works," *Time*, December 20, 2012, http://ti.me/11h4LEN. • **"It's also an issue of the kinds of communities that we're building"** Kathleen Hennessey, "In Chicago, Obama Talks of Community, Family in Curbing Violence," *Los Angeles Times*, February 15, 2013, http://lat.ms/11h56an.

THE WAY FORWARD

PAGE 154: " **'Hell will be forever for rent' "** Philip P. Mason, *Rum Running and the Roaring Twenties* (Detroit: Wayne State University Press, August 1, 1995), 36. • **"30,000–100,000 such clubs opened in the first five years in New York City alone"** "Teaching with Documents: The Volstead Act and Related Prohibition Documents," *archives.gov*, accessed March 15, 2013, http://1.usa.gov/11h5buJ. • " **'They carried hip flasks, hollowed canes, false books, and the like' "** "Teaching with Documents: The Volstead Act and Related Prohibition Documents," *archives.gov*, accessed March 15, 2013, http://1.usa.gov/11h5buJ. • **PAGE 155:** **"a felony punishable by up to ten years in prison"** Caroline May, "Biden to NRA: We 'Don't Have Time' to Prosecute Gun Buyers Who Lie on Background Checks," *dailycaller.com*, January 18, 2013, http://bit.ly/11h5m9k. • " **'prosecutors pursued just 44' "** Caroline May, "Biden to NRA: We 'Don't Have Time' to Prosecute Gun Buyers Who Lie on Background

Checks," *dailycaller.com*, January 18, 2013, http://bit.ly/11h5m9k. • **PAGE 156:** " 'that answers a question inaccurately' " Caroline May, "Biden to NRA: We 'Don't Have Time' to Prosecute Gun Buyers Who Lie on Background Checks," *dailycaller.com*, January 18, 2013, http://bit.ly/11h5m9k. • **have been judged mentally ill"** Joseph Tanfani, "Many Mentally Ill Missing from Gun Background Check System," *Los Angeles Times*, January 12, 2013, http://lat.ms/11h5wxv. • **"yet to report much of anything,"** Joseph Tanfani, "Many Mentally Ill Missing from Gun Background Check System," *Los Angeles Times*, January 12, 2013, http://lat.ms/11h5wxv. • " 'fewer than 100 records of individuals disqualified on mental health grounds' " Cory Booker, "It's Time to Emphasize Pragmatic and Achievable Gun Law Reform," *The Blog* blog at *huffingtonpost.com*, December 21, 2012, http://huff.to/11h74rn. • **PAGE 157:** " 'appropriated just 5.3 percent of the total authorized amount' " Matt MacBradaigh, "6 Biggest Problems with Mandatory Gun Background Checks," *policymic.com*, February 25, 2013, http://bit.ly/11h5GFa. • " 'which carries the *same punishment as trafficking chicken or livestock*' "Mathew T. Ryan, "Pass Commonsense Laws to Stop Gun Violence Now," *The Blog* blog at *huffingtonpost.com*, January 15, 2013, http://huff.to/11h6ZUL. • **"got their gun somewhere other than a retail store"** Matt MacBradaigh, "6 Biggest Problems with Mandatory Gun Background Checks," *policymic.com*, February 25, 2013, http://bit.ly/11h5GFa. • **PAGE 158:** " 'than be needed and not be here' " Scott Stump, "Town Puts Police Officers in Schools at No Cost to Taxpayers," *The Today Show*, NBC, March 6, 2013, http://on.today.com/11h5MwA. • **"it's still important for parents to understand how they work"** Andy Chalk, "Inappropriate Content: A Brief History of Videogame Ratings and the ESRB," *escapist magazine.com*, July 20, 2007, http://bit.ly/11h6mdJ. • **PAGE 159:** " 'scenes of intense violence, graphic sexual content and/or gambling with real currency' " "ESRB Ratings Guide," *esrb.org*, accessed March 15, 2013, http://bit.ly/11h6x8X. • **"the manufacturer blurred some of the worst scenes"** Ben Kuchera, "Edited, Smeared Manhunt 2 Kills Show in Video Form," *arstechnica.com*, October 26, 2007, http://ars .to/11h6rhC. • **"also has an M rating"** "Manhunt 2," Rockstar Games, as found for sale at Amazon.com, accessed March 19, 2013, http://amzn.to/YpNklW. • " 'sexual content and/or strong language' " "ESRB Ratings Guide," *esrb.org*, accessed March 15, 2013, http://bit.ly/11h6x8X. • **PAGE 160:** " 'minimal blood, simulated gambling and/or infrequent use of strong language' " "ESRB Ratings Guide," *esrb.org*, accessed March 15, 2013, http://bit.ly/11h6x8X. • " 'mild violence and/or infrequent use of mild language' " "ESRB Ratings Guide," *esrb.org*, accessed March 15, 2013, http://bit.ly/11h6x8X. • **PAGE 161:** "TV 'budget' or 'diet' " Sonia Tinsley and Tara Gallien, "Student Media Awareness to Reduce Television (SMART)," *gethealthycenla .org*, accessed March 15, 2013, http://bit.ly/11h6M3V. • **PAGE 162:** " 'Only community and parents and teachers and clergy can fill that hole' " President Barack Obama, "Remarks by the President on Strengthening the Economy for the Middle Class," Office of the Press Secretary, The White House, February 15, 20013, http://1 .usa.gov/11h6FFn.